Rediscovering Growth

# PERSPECTIVES

## Series editor: Diane Coyle

# Rediscovering Growth
## After the Crisis

Andrew Sentance

LONDON PUBLISHING PARTNERSHIP

Published by London Publishing Partnership
www.londonpublishingpartnership.co.uk

ISBN: 978-1-907994-15-9 (pbk.)

A catalogue record for this book is
available from the British Library

This book has been composed in Candara

Copy-edited and typeset by
T&T Productions Ltd, London

Cover design: Kate Prentice

# Contents

# Preface

What has happened to economic growth? Where has it gone? Why are we not returning to previous growth trends which seemed so positive in the 1990s and earlier in the 2000s?

In the aftermath of the financial crisis, these questions are being asked across the Western world by governments, companies and the general public. Many businesses lack confidence about their future prospects in the absence of the drivers of growth which sustained them before the crisis. With sluggish economic and business growth, tax receipts are weak so governments too are struggling to contain public borrowing, reduce their debts and establish a clear direction for economic policy. And when employers and public authorities don't seem to have a positive view of the economic outlook, it is not surprising that the public also lacks confidence in the future.

The global financial crisis of 2008–9 has been a watershed for economic growth in most Western economies. Though forecasts are becoming more positive about a pick-up in growth in Europe and the United States in 2014, this still does not represent a return to pre-2007 trends. And it follows three years in which growth has been disappointing across the Western world. Indeed, if the OECD's latest economic forecasts are correct, none of the major G7 economies will grow by over 2% this year (2013).[1] Since 1980, the only previous time that happened was in 2008 and 2009 in the midst of the global financial crisis.

This book aims to shed light on the underlying forces shaping this difficult economic situation in the West. Its central thesis is that the major Western economies – in Europe and North America – have entered a New Normal of disappointing economic growth and heightened volatility. And there isn't a quick and easy escape path from this pattern. But that does not mean we should be pessimistic about the longer-term economic outlook – hence the title: *Rediscovering Growth*. There is hope of a return to a more stable and sustained world of economic growth if we can learn the right lessons from previous twists and turns in our economic fortunes and adapt them to the circumstances we now face in the early 21st century.

What are those lessons? The first is that well-functioning and flexible economies can and do regenerate themselves. The British economy – which I know best because I have been following its progress since I started studying economics nearly forty years ago – is a very good example. The UK economy expanded at an average rate of over 3% per annum from the late 1940s until the early 1970s and then appeared to hit a brick wall after the mid-1970s recession. UK economic growth between 1973 and 1982 averaged less than 1% per annum. Pessimism was rife in the early 1980s, and there was widespread social unrest. 364 economists wrote to the *Times* newspaper to protest at the failings of government economic policy. And yet the British economy achieved a remarkable turnaround in the 1980s and set off on another quarter century of 3% plus growth in which the size of our economy doubled. This new 'golden age' of economic growth was only brought to an end by the global financial crisis in 2007–8.

The second lesson, however, is more challenging. In order to get on a new growth path painful adjustments in our economies and societies may be necessary. And we cannot guarantee that the necessary changes will take place in countries where there may be strong political resistance to change. Japan provides a very good example of this. Japan has built its economic success on a very productive, efficient and dynamic manufacturing sector. But from the mid 1990s onwards it has been clear to many observers that Japan needed to reform its labour markets and develop a more productive services sector to complement its very successful manufacturing industry. To date this has not happened, and hence Japanese growth remains in the doldrums. For Japan, the inability to undertake these structural changes is a much more important factor holding back growth than the legacy of its financial crisis in the early 1990s.

There are many other examples of economies which have struggled to recover past glories because they could not make the adjustment required. For example, Spain, Italy and Portugal, which flourished in the 1400s and 1500s, were overtaken by the major northern European powers including Britain, and have struggled ever since to re-establish their economic prowess.

The third lesson is that we should not expect the next growth phase to be like the last one. In the 1950s and 1960s, growth in the Western world was boosted by post-war reconstruction, an emerging middle class in Europe and North America, and the new technologies which had emerged in the 1920s, 1930s and during World War II. The development of mass markets for consumer products like motor cars, washing machines and transistor radios were key features of this post-war growth phase. The next growth phase, which started in the 1980s and developed momentum in the 1990s, was supported by a very different set of forces: financial deregulation and liberalization; the opening up of the world economy; and the revolution in information and communications technology which brought us the Internet and mobile phones.

It is not possible to pinpoint exactly what might drive a new growth phase which could become established later this decade. The experience of previous growth phases can offer only limited insights – we need to look forward rather than back to the past to identify potential new technologies and emerging business and consumer trends. But there are common conditions which have underpinned the two major growth phases we have seen in the modern post-war era – a supportive financial system and confidence in the stability and sustainability of economic policy. These preconditions do not yet seem to be in place to support a return to stronger growth in the major Western economies, though they could be later this decade.

The final lesson I would highlight from past experience is that some countries and some businesses have been much better at riding the changing tides of economic growth than others. Northern Europe – including the UK – has been an economic powerhouse for the world economy for at least three centuries now. North America and other offshoots of European civilisation developed and flourished in the 19th and 20th centuries – led by the United States. And it looks likely that the Asia–Pacific region – led by China and India – will be the driving force for the world economy in the 21st century. Looking ahead, we should expect these three regions to continue to provide the main support for economic growth across the world economy. Elsewhere, economic prospects look more uncertain and more variable.

The purpose of this book is to shed light on the big tides which underpin economic growth – not to provide detailed forecasts for GDP this year, next year or five years hence. I hope it will provide a map to help readers navigate the changing tides of economic fortune – and to prosper and succeed in these turbulent times.

In Chapter 1, I discuss how the global financial crisis of 2007–8 brought us down to earth after excessively optimistic assessments of economic prospects for the major Western economies in the mid 2000s. Chapter 2 looks back to the experience of the 1970s and highlights some uncanny parallels with our recent experience. In my view far too much reference has been made to the Great Depression of the 1930s in the economic analysis of the financial crisis, and not enough has been learned from the more recent economic and financial turbulence in the 1970s. That leads on to my view that we are in a New Normal of disappointing economic growth and volatility which is likely to persist for a while. That is the subject of Chapter 3.

The next two chapters discuss which countries will be the winners and losers in this brave new world (Chapter 4) and how governments might adapt their economic policies to the New Normal economic environment (Chapter 5). This leads on to a discussion in Chapter 6 of the potential drivers of business success in the post-crisis economic environment.

Chapter 7 focuses on how the major Western economies might exit from this rather disappointing phase in our economic journey. One view is that we can't or won't. But I think this is too fatalistic. The successful economies in the 21st century will be those which are prepared to embark on a new phase of economic reform and restructuring – and which recognize that the drivers of a future 'new growth phase' will need to be different from the past.

The final chapter discusses whether we should be optimists or pessimists about the economic outlook. I will not tell you here. You need to read the rest of the book to find out!

Chapter 1

# The end of the
# Great Stability

Our economic world changed dramatically in 2008 – a year which must go down as one of the most turbulent in the modern history of the global economy. The first half of the year was dominated by a strong surge in energy, food and other commodity prices – with the oil price rising to a peak of $147/barrel in July. Inflation and business costs were pushed up in most countries around the world, squeezing consumers and putting pressure on company finances. In the second half of the year, we experienced the full force of the financial crisis, which had been gathering momentum for over a year. Extreme turbulence in the financial system led to the failure of Lehman Brothers in September 2008 and the near collapse of other banks and financial institutions. Around the world, governments and central banks were forced to step in with bailouts and a raft of other emergency measures to prevent a total meltdown of the financial system.

Two years before this financial turmoil was unleashed in the autumn of 2008, I had left my job as Chief Economist at British Airways (BA) and joined the Bank of England Monetary Policy Committee (MPC) – the body which sets interest rates for the UK economy. While there was some discussion of financial risks on the MPC, the main focus of the economic debate in 2006 and 2007 was not on how unstable the economy might become, but why it had been so stable for so long. The prevailing view at that time was that the United Kingdom and other Western economies were experiencing a period of Great Stability – characterized by steady sustained growth and low inflation.

I joined the MPC just as this period of stability was coming to an end. With hindsight, I should have been prepared for that as turbulent economic conditions had been following me around throughout my career. I started my first job as an economist at the Confederation of British Industry (CBI) in 1986, just at the start of the major boom–bust cycle which dominated the late 1980s and early 1990s. I was responsible for the CBI's economic commentary and policy recommendations over a period which saw double-digit inflation, interest rates at 15%, a major recession, record public borrowing and the trauma of the United Kingdom leaving the European Exchange Rate Mechanism (ERM) less than two years after joining.

This pattern was repeated during my time at BA from 1998 to 2006 – which included the most severe downturn in the history of global aviation following the 9/11 attacks on the World Trade Centre. This massive shock to the airline industry threatened the survival of BA, and radical business surgery was needed to achieve a turnaround – including the loss of 13,000 jobs, nearly a quarter of the company's total workforce.

So perhaps I should not have been surprised when the early signs of the financial crisis began to emerge after less than a year of my time at the Bank of England. As the minutes for the August 2007 MPC meeting recorded:

> The main news this month in financial markets had been the sharp deterioration in credit markets and the associated

falls in equity prices and changes in market interest rates. A trigger for this turbulence appeared to be renewed concerns about the US sub-prime mortgage market, the losses of some prominent hedge funds, and the revisions to the ratings of some mortgage-backed securities; this had led to a reduction in demand for products such as sub-prime mortgage-backed securities and collateralised debt obligations.... It was not clear how far the downturn in financial markets would go, nor how long it would persist.

These financial market tensions led to the demise of the UK bank Northern Rock in the autumn of 2007 and major banks like Merrill Lynch, Citibank and UBS started to announce large losses and debt write-downs. Yet, at the start of 2008, views about the growth of the world economy remained remarkably positive. The IMF's January 2008 economic update predicted that the world economy would grow on average by over 4% in the coming calendar year. That would have been a healthy rate of growth by longer-term historical standards, even though it represented a slowdown from the boom-time global economic conditions of 2004–7.[2]

A year later, in January 2009, in the aftermath of the collapse of Lehman Brothers and all the other financial turbulence in autumn 2008, things looked very different. The outlook was for recession across the world economy with sharp declines in output in all the major Western economies. Under the headline 'Global Economic Slump Challenges Policies', the IMF predicted that world growth would be just 0.5% in the year ahead, the weakest year for global growth since 1950 at least.[3] In fact this was an underestimate of the scale of the downturn – world GDP actually fell in 2009 for the first time since World War II.

Going back to the start of the 20th century, there are only two other peacetime years when the outlook for the world economy deteriorated as dramatically as in 2008. One is 1930, which marked the onset of a prolonged depression in the United States and Europe after the Wall Street Crash of 1929, bringing to an end the prosperity of the 'roaring twenties'. The other is 1974, when the long post-war boom came to an end amidst rampant inflation, rocketing oil prices and financial turbulence. That year ushered in a long period of economic turmoil in many economies which continued until the mid-1980s.

## The Great Stability

As in the 1930s and the mid 1970s, policymakers were unprepared for the big change in the economic climate in the late 2000s. The long period of healthy growth and low inflation since the early 1990s had led to the expectation that big swings in the economy were a thing of the past. In his 2004 Budget speech, the UK Chancellor of the Exchequer Gordon Brown proclaimed:

> Britain is enjoying its longest period of sustained economic growth for more than 200 years... the longest period of sustained growth since the beginning of the Industrial Revolution.[4]

This optimistic assessment reflected the positive performance of the British economy since the early 1990s. UK economic growth averaged 3.3% per annum between 1993 and 2007 – very impressive by past historical comparisons and in line with the growth rate Britain had achieved in the post-war golden age from the late 1940s until the early 1970s. Even in the weakest year for UK economic growth between 1993 and 2007 – in 2002 – GDP grew by 2.4%, despite a weak global economy in the aftermath of the 9/11 attacks. (This 'weak' GDP rise in 2002 is still stronger than any year of growth we have seen so far since the financial crisis!)

Alongside this healthy rate of economic growth, low and stable inflation reinforced the widespread perception of economic stability. For two decades, from the early 1970s until the early 1990s, UK policymakers had battled to subdue inflation. The annual rate of increase in prices had hit a peak of nearly 27% in the summer of 1975 – averaging over 13% in the 1970s and running at 6% through the 1980s. But from 1993 until 2007 – with monetary policy explicitly targeting a low and stable rate of inflation – the British economy enjoyed its longest and most sustained period of price stability since World War II.[5] The establishment of the Bank of England Monetary Policy Committee in 1997, with independent control over monetary policy, reinforced the view that low inflation was now institutionalized in the United Kingdom. The Governor of the Bank of England was expected to write an explanatory letter to the Chancellor of the Exchequer if inflation deviated more than one percentage point from the target. When I joined the MPC in the autumn of 2006, nearly a decade had elapsed without one of these letters being written – though the first was despatched in March 2007, and thirteen more have been written since then!

The United Kingdom was not the only economy experiencing these benign economic conditions. In the United States, there was also a belief that their economy had entered a prolonged period of sustained growth and low inflation known as the 'Great Moderation'. Like the United Kingdom, this view was reinforced by a high degree of confidence in the ability of the central bank to maintain sustained economic growth and stable prices. In the early 2000s, under its chairman Alan Greenspan, the US Federal Reserve had cut interest rates aggressively to steer the US economy away from recession when the dotcom US stock market bubble burst. And in the mid 2000s there was great confidence in the ability of Greenspan's successor, Ben Bernanke, to do something similar if the situation demanded it. Meanwhile, the establishment of the euro as a single currency was seen as a stabilizing force for the European economy – anchored by a European Central Bank modelled on the Deutsche Bundesbank, which had successfully held back inflationary pressures and countered economic volatility in the 1970s and 1980s.

Reflecting the mood of these times, the Bank of England hosted a major international conference in September 2007 aimed at understanding the sources of macroeconomic stability.[6] It was highly ironic that as economists and policymakers gathered in London to understand why Western economies had become so stable, confidence in the Great Stability was being undermined on the streets of cities and towns across the United Kingdom. Queues were forming outside branches of Northern Rock as customers sought to take their money out of the bank. When the Bank of England and the UK government appreciated the severity of the crisis, they intervened to rescue Northern Rock. But a year later, in the autumn of 2008, the financial turbulence hit other much larger banks – including Royal Bank of Scotland, HBOS, Citibank and Lehman Brothers. By then, it was clear then that the era of the Great Stability had already come to an end.


## The Global Financial Crisis: A rude awakening

The financial crisis of 2008–9 provided a rude awakening from excessively optimistic views about our ability to maintain a long and sustained period of economic growth. It was also a reminder that, however adept national economic authorities were, developments in the global economy were a potential source of economic instability. Indeed, even before I joined the MPC in 2006, it was clear that international rather than domestic factors were the main sources of volatility driving changes in UK monetary policy.

The MPC was established in 1997 just before the onset of the Asian financial crisis, which threatened the growth of the global economy. This was followed in the late 1990s and early 2000s by the dotcom boom and bust which had its roots in excessive optimism about the ability of information technology and the Internet to transform the prospects of the US economy. The weakness of the global economy in the early 2000s was reinforced by international political instability following the 9/11 attacks and then war in Afghanistan and Iraq. But just as the world economy emerged from this period of turbulence, we started to see surges in global energy and commodity prices. The price of oil, which had been stable at around $20/barrel for most of the 1990s and early 2000s surged to over $50/barrel in 2004 and hit $80/barrel in 2006 just before I joined the MPC. Two years later it had reached nearly $150/barrel.

When facing global shocks of this sort, a central bank in a single country like the United Kingdom can only do a limited amount to offset their economic impact. As long as the shocks are not too big, it is possible to keep the economy on a reasonably steady growth and low inflation track – which is what happened in most Western economies through the period from 1993 until 2007. But the global financial crisis exposed the limits of the ability of national authorities to stabilize economies in the face of such a severe global economic shock. Even though interest rates were cut to rock bottom levels and other emergency measures taken to stabilize the financial system around the world, a major world recession could not be avoided. Between 2007 and 2009, GDP fell in the G7 economies by over 4%, with the decline varying between 1.7% (Canada) and 6.6% (Italy and Japan) – leading to a rise in unemployment rose around the world.

To counter this severe economic downturn, policymakers unleashed a whole raft of measures to provide emergency support to their economies and stabilize the financial system. Governments took financial stakes in banks and allowed their borrowing to rise to cover this. Central banks cut official interest rates to rock-bottom levels. In the United Kingdom, the Bank Rate of 0.5% we set in March 2009 is the lowest seen in recorded history – lower even than in the Great Depression of the 1930s when the official rate of interest did not fall below 2%. Money was also injected into economies through central bank purchases of government bonds and other assets – under a policy with the unappetizing title of quantitative easing. And for a while governments were prepared to increase their spending and cut taxes to support a return to growth.

These policies succeeded in heading off a downward spiral in the global economy. But they have achieved only limited success in terms of a return to economic growth. In the Western world, economic stimulus has produced a recovery but 'not as we know it' (to adapt a famous quotation from *Star Trek*).[7] Even allowing for some pick-up in 2014, growth in the major Western economies has not returned to the previous trend rate experienced before the recession, as Figure 1.1 shows. The only exception to this pattern is Germany, where growth was relatively subdued before the crisis.

On average, the seven largest Western economies (the G7 nations excluding Japan plus Spain) grew by 2.7% per annum in the decade before the financial crisis. In the first five years of economic recovery, 2010–14, the same group of economies

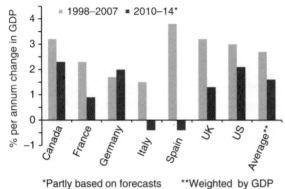

Figure 1.1. Western growth pre- and post-crisis.
*Source*: IMF, updated with PwC forecasts.

is likely to grow at just over half that rate, even allowing for some growth rebound in 2014. The slowdown is less marked in North America than in the major European economies. And countries in southern Europe have seen the biggest deterioration in economic performance.

This is not just disappointing performance by comparison with the pre-2007 growth period. It is also slow growth by comparison with previous economic recoveries in the major Western economies. Average economic growth in the United States in the first five years of this recovery (2010–14) is expected to be 2.2% per annum, compared with 3.8% and 3.3% in the equivalent phases of the 1980s and 1990s recoveries. In the four major European economies, the IMF expects to see annual growth of just 0.9% in the period 2010–14, which is around half the growth rate achieved in the equivalent five years in the 1980s and 1990s (2.0% and 1.6%).

The global financial crisis has clearly played a part in contributing to this experience of slow growth – both in terms of the big shock it delivered to many economies and the impact it has had on access to finance. The pre-2007 world of 'easy money' – in which the financial system was providing a substantial tailwind to economic growth – has been replaced by a much more cautious and restricted banking system in many countries. But this change in the financial climate has not been the only factor at work. In Chapter 3 we will discuss how a combination of economic headwinds is contributing to this New Normal of disappointing economic growth in the West. There are, however, a number of myths and misperceptions have grown up about the reasons for disappointing growth in the major Western economies. And it is helpful to dispel some of these at the outset.

## Myth 1: Global growth is weak

The first myth is that disappointing growth in the major Western economies reflects a weak global economy more generally. That is not true. Across the world economy as a whole, real economic growth is averaging close to 4% over the course of this recovery[8] – not as strong as the peak years in the mid 2000s when the world economy was booming, but very respectable by comparison with historical trends. The slowdown experienced in the West has not been shared by the leading emerging market economies, as Figure 1.2 shows. In the emerging and developing world, economies have generally bounced back to the strong rates of growth they were experiencing before the crisis. Indeed, the IMF is expecting the same rate of growth in the emerging market and developing economies in the five years to 2014 as we saw in the decade to 2007 – nearly 6% per annum.

In the immediate aftermath of the financial crisis, there was also a concern that the world economy would lapse into deflation – a situation where the money value of spending

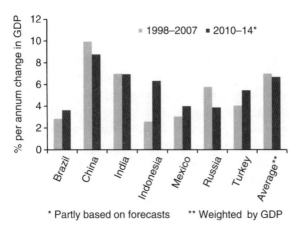

* Partly based on forecasts      ** Weighted by GDP

Figure 1.2. Robust growth in emerging economies.
*Source*: IMF World Economic Outlook.

stagnates or declines and where prices fall. Deflation was a feature of the depression of the 1930s, with US consumer prices falling by a quarter between 1930 and 1933. But these fears have not been borne out; instead the value of world economic output continues to expand, measured in terms of its most widely used currency, the US dollar. At the start of this century, the total value of economic activity in the world economy was $32 trillion. By 2008, this figure had near-ly doubled to $61 trillion, a remarkably rapid rate of progress, averaging over 8% a year. After a brief dip in 2009, the size of the world economy has now expanded to an estimated $74 trillion in 2013. And by 2018, the IMF estimates that world GDP will be worth $97 trillion – around three times as much as at the turn of the century.

Despite a major global financial upheaval, the money value of output in the world economy has tripled in size in less than two decades. And it is inflation rather than deflation that has been the bigger problem as a result. This has been particularly

11

true in emerging markets and developing economies, where growth has been strongest and consumer prices have risen on average by 6–7% in each of the last three years. One of the key drivers of inflation across the world economy in recent years has been rising energy, food and commodity prices. Since the early 2000s, whenever there has been a sustained pick-up in global growth, we have also seen a surge in the price of oil and many other commodities traded on world markets, including foodstuffs. This has happened repeatedly: in 2003–5, 2006–8 and in 2010–11.

In the major Western economies this has created bursts of the 'wrong' sort of inflation. We have been used to seeing inflation as a by-product of strong growth in our own economies. But imported inflation from rising energy and commodity prices squeezes consumers and business profits and hence acts as a dampener to growth in the short term. This squeeze has aggravated the problem of sustaining recovery since the financial crisis. And in countries which have seen a large fall in their exchange rate – like the United Kingdom – a devalued currency has added to the rise in imported inflation and the pressures on consumers to hold back spending.

## Myth 2: Fiscal austerity to blame

A second myth that has grown up around disappointing Western growth is that it is primarily due to austerity – a squeeze on public spending and/or higher taxation – as governments seek to reduce their borrowing and debt levels. This view is particularly prevalent in the United Kingdom and in a number of other European countries, where efforts to restrain public spending have attracted a lot of news coverage and public debate.

It is true that government spending has not being contributing to growth in recent years. That is not a great surprise. Public borrowing levels were allowed to rise sharply in 2008–9 as the downturn eroded tax receipts and public spending was boosted in many countries to stabilize the economy. In 2009, public borrowing reached nearly 12% of GDP in the United States, 11% in the United Kingdom and over 6% of the national output of the euro area economies. These are unsustainable levels of borrowing which have pushed up government debt sharply and a period of spending restraint is therefore needed to restore stability.

But the notion that government spending is dragging down growth through austerity, either in the Western economies more generally, in the euro area or the United Kingdom, is misleading. Figure 1.3 shows that for the OECD economies as a group[9], for the euro area and for the United Kingdom, real government spending on goods and services has been broadly flat after increasing quite significantly in 2008–9. The country where government spending has been cut back most noticeably in real terms is the United States. And yet the United States has been one of the better-performing

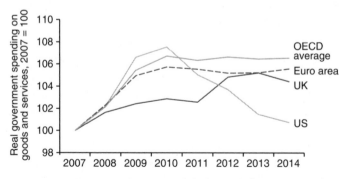

Figure 1.3. Public expenditure in advanced economies. *Source*: OECD Economic Outlook.

Western economies in recent years, which casts further doubt on the view that fiscal austerity is responsible for weak growth.

The main source of the weakness of growth of demand in the Western economies is not from the public sector but from private consumer spending. There are various ways through which lower public spending can affect the willingness of consumers to spend – through its impact on public sector pay and the payment of pensions and benefits – but this does not appear to be the major cause of weak consumer spending. Nor can higher taxes be blamed – across the OECD economies the average tax burden as a share of GDP in 2013–14 is no higher than in 2007–8. There are other more important factors which have been squeezing consumers and making them more reluctant to spend, which are discussed in Chapter 3.

## Myth 3: Not enough monetary stimulus

So if governments are not to blame for weak Western growth, what about central bankers? Could monetary policy have done more to restore growth to its previous trend? As we discussed above, monetary policy was used very aggressively in the depths of the financial crisis in 2008–9 to combat the negative trends in the major economies of the Western world. Official interest rates were reduced to near-zero levels across Europe and in North America. Beyond that, central banks have inflated their balance sheets as they have sought to pump money into the economy by purchasing government bonds and other assets. Former Goldman Sachs Chief Economist Gavyn Davies estimates that total central bank assets and liabilities have more than doubled in size in relation to the world economy since the early 2000s – rising from 14% of world GDP then to 32% now.[10] The bulk of this expansion took place in response to the financial crisis.

Initially, these policies were successful as they stabilized economic and financial conditions and provided the basis of a recovery starting in the second half of 2009. But subsequent efforts to reinvigorate growth since 2010 with further rounds of quantitative easing in the United States and the United Kingdom have not worked. The US Federal Reserve launched its 'QE2' policy in late 2010 and continued it through the first half of 2011. But this did not prevent the US growth rate slowing down to below 2% per annum in 2011. A further round of asset purchases which started in mid-2012 – 'QE3' – also appears to have had a limited effect on economic growth rates. In the same way, additional injections of quantitative easing by the Bank of England in late 2011 and 2012 did not prevent the economy slowing to almost a standstill over that period.

Some argue that the outcomes in the United States and the United Kingdom would have been even worse without these injections of additional money or that lags in the system have delayed their impact. I would dispute these arguments. But, in any case, these continuing programmes of central bank stimulus have clearly not been able to restore the growth rate back to its pre-crisis trend. This is in line with the consensus view of economists since the 1980s that monetary policy is best suited to ironing out short-term fluctuations in the economy and does not have the potential to influence growth trends over longer periods. Longer-term growth reflects deeper fundamentals relating to the capabilities of our economies – the capacity of businesses to innovate and develop new products and processes, their confidence in investing in new facilities, the skills of the workers they employ, and their ability to provide the goods and services which the public demand.

## The reality: It's the New Normal

A common theme underpinning these myths and misperceptions about our problem of slow growth in the West is that there is an external force holding our economies back. So if only that dampening influence could be removed, growth could bounce back to the rates we enjoyed before the crisis. In other words, if the world economy picked up, if the government abandoned austerity, or if central banks were able to do more – everything would be all right.

But that is not the case – which is now being more widely recognized. The forces shaping our New Normal of disappointing growth in the Western world are more deeply rooted within our economies and cannot be relieved easily. As a result, we need to be more willing to adapt to our current situation and take a longer-term view of how we might improve economic prospects. But before we turn to a more in-depth analysis of our New Normal economy, it makes sense to consider the lessons of history.

In the words of the Spanish philosopher George Santayana: 'Those who cannot remember the past are condemned to repeat it.' So the next chapter considers what we can learn from the two previous episodes when we have seen serious financial and economic turmoil in the major Western economies and a big dislocation of growth: the 1930s and the 1970s.

Chapter 2

# Lessons from the past

B efore 2008, there were only two previous years in modern peacetime history which saw such a dramatic turning point in the world economy: 1930 and 1974. Both years
ushered in a prolonged period of disappointing economic
growth, high unemployment and turbulence across the major
economies of the Western world. What lessons can we draw
from these previous episodes?

In responding to the recent financial crisis, policymakers
and commentators have tended to draw more heavily on the
experience of the 1930s than the 1970s. Ben Bernanke, the
outgoing Chairman of the US Federal Reserve, studied the
1930s' experience as an academic. In a speech in April 2010,[11]
he highlighted four key lessons from that period:

> First, economic prosperity depends on financial stability;
> second, policymakers must respond forcefully, creatively,
> and decisively to severe financial crises; third, crises that are
> international in scope require an international response; and
> fourth, unfortunately, history is never a perfect guide.

The former Governor of the Bank of England, Mervyn King,
was an academic colleague of Bernanke's in the United States
in the early 1980s. In a speech thirty years later,[12] he referred

back to that experience in highlighting the lessons he drew from the experience of the 1930s:

> Thirty years ago Ben Bernanke and I had adjoining offices at MIT. We never imagined that thirty years later we would be colleagues as central bank governors, and even if we had, we would never have believed that the industrialised world would have faced an economic and financial crisis on a par with the problems seen in the 1930s... The worst problems of the 1930s were avoided this time around because of the stimulatory policies injected into the world economy by central banks and governments around the world although it is fair to say that a recovery of a durable kind is proving elusive.

## Lessons from the 1930s

The analysis of the Great Depression by Bernanke and others – building on earlier research by Milton Friedman and Anna Schwartz[13] – highlighted the importance of a large monetary contraction as a key factor triggering the depression of the 1930s. This monetary squeeze was aggravated by the efforts of countries to stay on the Gold Standard, which locked them into a deflationary downward spiral. In 1931, Britain and a number of other countries abandoned the link to gold, but it was not until the beginning of 1934 that the United States devalued the dollar relative to the gold price. By that time its unemployment rate had already risen to over 20%. Meanwhile US GDP fell by nearly 30% in real terms between 1929 and 1933, and the level of prices dropped by around a quarter over the same period. The rise in unemployment and the fall in output and prices were much less pronounced in countries like the United Kingdom which had abandoned the Gold Standard more quickly.

The key driving force behind the policy measures taken around the world in late 2008 and 2009 was to avoid a repeat of this dismal record of economic failure. And this was successfully achieved. Although GDP fell and unemployment rose, the very severe distress of the 1930s was avoided. As Figure 2.1 shows, the levels of unemployment experienced in the United States, United Kingdom and Europe were much closer to the experience of previous post-war recessions – in the 1980s and 1990s – than they were to the 1930s.

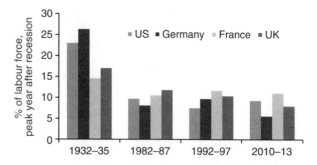

Figure 2.1. Post-recession unemployment rates. *Source*: IMF from 1980; various historical studies for 1930s.

Other problems which had contributed to the severity of the depression in the 1930s were also avoided following the recent financial crisis. Deflation has not emerged as a serious phenomenon. As we noted in Chapter 1, inflation has been a bigger problem since the financial crisis than falling prices – particularly in emerging market economies. Fiscal policies have also been more flexible. When the recession hit in 2008–9, governments were prepared to allow their deficits to rise for a while and incur extra borrowing to support demand – heeding the policy advice from John Maynard Keynes in the 1930s. It is only as growth has resumed that Western governments have focused more actively on deficit and debt reduction.

Another important difference from the 1930s is that we have seen a stronger focus on international economic policy cooperation, which was particularly noticeable in the depths of the crisis in 2008 and 2009. The G20 – which includes leading emerging markets and developing economies as well as the major Western powers – has become an important forum for discussion of international economic policy issues. The G20 Summit in London in April 2009 provided a strong commitment to use expansionary monetary policies across the world to support demand and to avoid protectionism, even though there were differences of view and emphasis between governments on how far extra public spending and borrowing should be used to support demand.

Perhaps most important of all, the world has avoided a serious lapse into protectionism, which greatly aggravated the length and depth of the Great Depression. The US Tariff Act, which was signed into law in June 1930, prompted a worldwide surge in protectionist measures as other countries retaliated to restrictions on their exports. World trade fell between 1929 and 1933 by nearly 30% and trade volumes did not recover their pre-recession level until after World War II.[14]

By contrast, though world trade was hit by recession in 2008–9, it soon bounced back. Trade volumes dropped by more than 10% in 2009, but that decline was more than recouped in 2010 and world trade in 2013 is, at the time of writing, estimated to be 13% above its pre-recession peak in 2008. There have been occasional bouts of sabre rattling on trade issues – like the spat in 2013 between the European Union and China over the alleged dumping of solar panels. There have also been periodic concerns about so-called currency wars – worries that competitive devaluations would spur a round of protectionist responses with new trade barriers being imposed. But the open rule-based trade system policed by the

World Trade Organization (WTO) has been kept intact. Indeed, more countries and people are actively participating in the world trading system than at any previous time in the history of the world. The WTO currently has 159 member countries which account for over 98% of global trade and GDP and around 94% of the world's population.

So if the lessons of the 1930s have been heeded and have had a major influence on policymaking, what about the lessons of the 1970s? The economic turmoil we saw then has been a less obvious point of reference for policymakers and economic analysts recently – perhaps because that decade is remembered, particularly in Britain, as a time of rip-roaring inflation. Even though inflation has been higher than expected in many countries in recent years, it has not become the dominant economic problem that it was for major economies like the United Kingdom and the United States in the 1970s. But this important difference has deflected attention away from other parallels between our current position and the 1970s. Economically, we have gone back to the 70s in four significant ways.

## Back to the 70s: Financial crisis

As in 2008, an international financial crisis – with its roots in the policies pursued by the United States – paved the way for the economic turmoil of the mid 1970s and beyond. Unlike our recent crisis, the financial turbulence of the early 1970s did not originate from instability in banks and other private sector financial institutions. It stemmed from the unravelling of the official framework underpinning financial stability – the system of fixed exchange rates which had been in place for a quarter of a century after World War II.

21

This set of arrangements – known as the Bretton Woods system – provided a vital anchor for the long post-war expansion which dominated the 1950s and 1960s in Europe and North America.

The Bretton Woods system derives its name from a town in New Hampshire in the United States where the Allied nations met in 1944 to plan for the post-war economic future, amid growing confidence that they would be victorious in World War II. The objective was to put in place a more cooperative system of international finance and economic policymaking to avoid the problems which had plagued the world's major economies in the 1930s. The great economist John Maynard Keynes played a major role in the conference – though not all his ideas were adopted.

There were three main elements of the Bretton Woods system: the establishment of the International Monetary Fund (IMF); the creation of the World Bank; and a commitment to maintain a system of fixed exchange rates linked to the US dollar, which was in turn pegged to the value of gold. It was the fixed currency system anchored to a stable, low-inflation US economy which was the most important element of Bretton Woods, even though there were occasional realignments (such as the United Kingdom's 1967 devaluation). And in the end, the role of the dollar and its link to gold turned out to be the key vulnerability. When the United States could no longer act as a guarantor of economic stability, the foundations of the system were undermined – exactly the scenario which unfolded in the early 1970s.

In August 1971, with its balance of payments and budget deficit under pressure because of the costs of the Vietnam War, the United States abandoned its currency link to the gold price. US inflation was also rising, and this combination of events undermined confidence in the dollar as the keystone for the global financial system. The system of fixed exchange rates which had underpinned two decades of post-war growth and stability then started to unravel. Though various attempts were made to restore a system of fixed exchange rates, in February 1973, Japan and the major European nations abandoned their link to the dollar and the world entered a period of floating exchange rates.

Economic policymakers, however, had come to rely on the underpinning provided by a fixed exchange rate regime linked to the US dollar. In its absence, the international financial system became very volatile and unstable in 1973 and 1974. Inflation rose, growth faltered and stock markets fell. The US equity market lost 45% of its value in 1973 and 1974 and the value of UK stocks and shares fell by a staggering 78%. There were also bank failures in the United Kingdom and Germany as the financial turmoil took hold. Volatile financial economic conditions persisted through the 1970s and into the 1980s – aggravated by domestic economic policy failures in some economies, including the United Kingdom. It was about a decade before more stable financial conditions re-emerged in the mid 1980s.

## Back to the 70s: Energy price shocks

A second similarity between our recent experience and the economic turbulence which hit in the 1970s was the role played by rising energy prices. Through the 1950s and 1960s, economic growth was supported by low energy prices as the oil supplies of the Middle East were exploited by large Western companies. To counter Western influence, OPEC (the Organization of Petroleum Exporting Companies) was established in 1960 and started to flex its economic muscle in the early 1970s. During the Yom Kippur war between Israel and Egypt in the autumn of 1973, OPEC started a series of price rises, backed by restrictions in output. The price of oil rose to 4–5 times its previous value, from $2–2.5/barrel in the early 1970s to $11–14/barrel from 1974 to 1978. There was a further increase to over $30/barrel in 1980, which was sustained until prices fell after 1985. In today's prices, oil prices were $50–100/barrel from 1974 until 1985 as Figure 2.2 shows. And it was only after twenty years – in the mid 2000s – that the oil price regained such a high level.

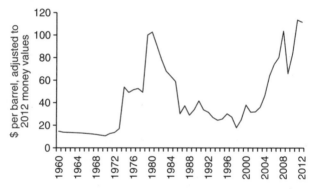

Figure 2.2. Crude oil price in real terms.
*Source*: BP Statistical Review of World Energy.

In the 1970s, oil price rises helped to fuel a wage–price spiral that contributed to the inflationary problems of that period. We have not seen that happen this time around. But in other respects, the economic impact of rising energy costs has been similar. Costs have risen, squeezing profits in energy-intensive industries. Consumers have faced rises in the prices of basic essentials (including food prices, which are highly sensitive to rising energy costs), reducing their ability to spend on more discretionary items.

**Back to the 70s: Growth slowdown**

Partly in response to this period of financial turmoil and big shocks to energy prices, the major Western economies experienced a sharp slowdown in economic growth in the 1970s, which is the third significant parallel with our recent experience. Like the United Kingdom, the major Western economies saw around a quarter of a century of virtually uninterrupted growth from the late 1940s until the early 1970s. Between 1948 and 1973, the economies of western Europe grew on average by 5% per annum and the United States grew by 4%. The UK economy appeared a relative laggard, with growth of just 3.3%. But by comparison with the years that followed, this was a golden age. Between 1973 and 1982, growth in western Europe slowed to 2% and the US growth rate was just 2.1%. In the United Kingdom, growth was a miserly 0.9% over this nine-year period – a lost decade for an economy which was once the workshop of the world.

In the 1980s, growth rates picked up again and we saw a renewed long period of economic expansion in Western economies continuing until the onset of the financial crisis – with the brief interruption of the early 1990s recession. But this was not a return to the pattern of growth we had left behind in the early 1970s. When growth re-emerged in the 1980s, the new drivers – in the service industries and the financial sector – were very different from the long expansion of the 1950s and 1960s, which had relied on post-war reconstruction and expanding markets for cars and other consumer durable goods.

As Figure 2.3 shows, the phase we are in now is akin to the 1973–82 period, except that growth rates have ratcheted down even further. Between 2007 and 2017 – according to the latest IMF forecasts – the economies of the European Union

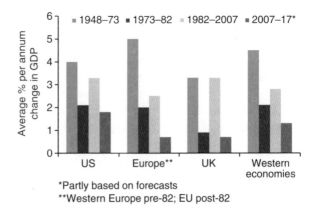

*Partly based on forecasts
**Western Europe pre-82; EU post-82

Figure 2.3. Growth phases in Western economies.
*Source*: Maddison Growth Project, ONS, IMF and PwC.

are projected to grow by just 0.6% per annum, and the UK economy will grow at a similar rate. The US economy is doing better – but even there growth is forecast by the IMF to average just 1.8% in the decade following the financial crisis.

If the experience of the 1970s and early 1980s is repeated, Western economies could return to a period of more sustained and stronger growth eventually. But after the shock of the 70s it took about ten years to complete the process of economic adjustment before a new growth phase began to emerge. It was not until the mid 1980s, about a decade after the 1973–4 crisis, that the major Western economies returned to a more sustained period of growth.

One of the reasons for this long process of adjustment is that big shocks to the global economic system bring other problems in their wake. In the 1930s the legacy was deflation and protectionism; in the 1970s it was inflation; and this time round it is the large deficits and debts which the financial crisis has bequeathed to governments. Until policymakers have properly addressed the problems created by the aftermath of a big shock to the economic system, private individuals and firms will not have the confidence to spend and invest which leads to a new self-sustaining and prolonged period of economic growth.

## Back to the 70s: Economic policy disrupted

This brings me to the final similarity between the recent financial crisis and the shocks to the world economy we experienced in the 1970s. On both occasions a stable economic policy regime which had previously appeared sustainable was disrupted. The relative stability of policy which underpinned the long expansion of the 1950s and 1960s was based on the notion that governments were able to maintain a new era of 'full employment' underpinned by a stable exchange rate regime. This gave way in the 1970s to a struggle to control inflation and high public deficits. Similarly, the prevailing view before the financial crisis that we had entered a new paradigm of economic stability has now given way to a series of emergency policy responses and a prolonged struggle to restore order to public finances.

When economies appear unstable and not properly under the control of the authorities, the private sector and financial markets will inevitably find it hard to maintain their confidence in economic prospects. In the 1970s, the main symptom of the lack of control of the economy was inflation. Inflation is clearly damaging in its own right – reducing the efficiency of the economy, adding to uncertainty and creating arbitrary redistributions of income. But just as damaging as these real effects is the perception that a key ingredient of broader economic stability – the stability of prices – is out of the control of the authorities.

Inflation was aggravated in the United Kingdom and some other economies by attempts to stimulate growth and restore the old world of full employment. Alongside the financial instability and energy price shocks in the mid 70s, this made the problem worse. As James Callaghan – British prime minister in the late 1970s – acknowledged in a speech to the Labour Party Conference in 1976:

> We used to think that you could spend your way out of a recession and increase employment by cutting taxes and boosting government spending. I tell you in all candour that that option no longer exists, and in so far as it ever did exist, it only worked on each occasion since the war by injecting a bigger dose of inflation into the economy, followed by a higher level of unemployment as the next step.

Callaghan's admission was the start of a serious attempt to get on top of inflation in the United Kingdom in the late 1970s and early 1980s, buttressed by the humiliating experience of having to call in the IMF in 1976 to provide emergency financial support. And by 1982–3, when inflation came down and government spending started to be brought under control, confidence began to return in the private sector. Other Western economies also saw a reduction in inflation and a return in confidence in the 1980s, which was associated with an improvement in economic growth and employment prospects.

Though high inflation is not the main problem for the Western economies in the aftermath of the global financial crisis of 2008–9, we are seeing a similar loss of confidence in the ability of the public authorities to restore stability to major economies. Before 2007, it appeared that sound public finances and sensible adjustments to monetary policy could keep economies on a steady-growth, low-inflation track. This no longer appears to be the case. Public sector deficits have expanded as governments sought to maintain spending while the recession was eroding tax receipts. This has pushed up the ratio of public sector debt to GDP sharply across the Western world – as Figure 2.4 shows. At the same time, central banks have sought to support growth with very low interest rates and regular injections of quantitative easing – leading to large purchases of government debt.

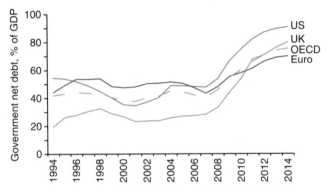

Figure 2.4. Public debt has risen sharply.
*Source*: OECD Economic Outlook.

While these policies can be justified as a response to severe short-term difficulties, they are not likely to be supportive of strong medium-term growth. Just like the response to the inflation of the 1970s, firms and individuals will not have the confidence to invest and spend when economic fundamentals do not appear to be on a sound footing. However, correcting government deficits and returning monetary policy settings to more normal levels in the current environment is not easy. It took policy-makers about a decade to get to grips with the problems of inflation and public finances in the 1970s and early 1980s. And it is likely to be an equally long haul to get back to more sustainable economic policies following the recent financial crisis.

These parallels with the 1970s suggest there is unlikely to be a quick escape from the current phase of disappointing Western growth. But history never repeats itself in exactly the same way. So to assess our future economic prospects in more depth, we need to understand in more detail the forces underpinning the current New Normal of slow growth. That is the subject of the next chapter.

Chapter 3

# The New Normal

Why has growth in the major Western economies been so disappointing since the financial crisis? In the first chapter of this book we dispelled a few myths – that the world economy as a whole is weak, that fiscal austerity is to blame and that monetary policy should have been used more aggressively.

We can also rule out some other potential culprits. Demographic factors are not the cause of the growth slowdown. Population growth across the G7 major economies is projected to slow slightly between the ten years before 2007 and the ten years after, as Figure 3.1 shows. But this is a very modest contribution to slower growth subtracting about 0.1% per annum from average G7 growth over the course of a decade. Populations in most Western economies are ageing, which has an additional negative impact on the growth of the labour force. But this is being offset by later retirement, increased female participation in the labour force and more flexible working. Across the G7 economies as a whole, the growth of the labour force is increasing broadly in line with population growth at around 0.5% per annum.[15]

The most striking thing about Figure 3.1 is the differences between rates of population growth in some of the major developed economies. In the decade 2007–17, the United

Kingdom, United States and Canada are expected to benefit from annual population growth of 0.8–1.1%, compared with –0.1% in Germany and –0.2% in Japan. These contrasting demographic trends play an important part in accounting for differences between economic growth prospects across the major Western economies, as we will discuss later in this book.

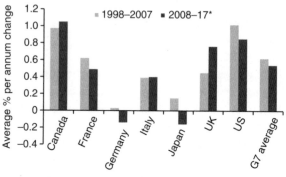

*Partly based on forecasts

Figure 3.1. Population growth in G7 economies.
*Source*: IMF World Economic Outlook.

Another explanation we can fairly easily dismiss is a slowing pace of technological change. Over the very long run, technology plays an important part in supporting economic growth – through the invention of new products as well as enabling more efficient ways of producing existing goods and services. Per capita economic growth was zero or negligible before the technological breakthroughs which started the industrial revolution in Britain in the 18th century. The last 250 years of economic growth across the Western world have been underpinned by a stream of new inventions and innovations – starting with the steam engine and the Spinning Jenny, and then continuing with the development of railways, motor cars, electrical power, aircraft and telephones. More recent advances in science and technology have led to rapid advances in medicine, the development of electrical and electronic goods, and the Internet.

Some economists such as Robert Gordon at NorthWestern University in the United States take a pessimistic view of future advances in technology. But there are few signs that this pace of technological change is slowing down.[16] Information and communications technology (e.g. mobile phones, the Internet, etc.) continues to progress and evolve. New materials are being developed and used to make products more efficient and lighter. For example, half of the airframe of the new Boeing 787 Dreamliner is constructed from carbon fibre instead of traditional metal. At the same time, revolutionary new materials are being developed – like graphene, a very thin and light carbon material. Meanwhile, biotechnology and genetic engineering are helping to push forward the frontiers of medical science and food production. There are also significant technological developments in the energy and transport industries – like solar and wind power and electric cars – which could aid the transition to a low-carbon society.

### Why has productivity slowed?

Though the pace of technological change may not have slackened, Western economies have found it more difficult to secure productivity growth in recent years. As Figure 3.2 shows, the pace of productivity growth (as measured by output per worker) across the G7 economies has fallen back sharply since the mid 2000s. No G7 economy is expected to achieve productivity growth of more than 1% per annum in the decade 2004–2014, whereas in the preceding two decades productivity growth averaged 2.1% (1984–94) and 1.6% (1994–2004).

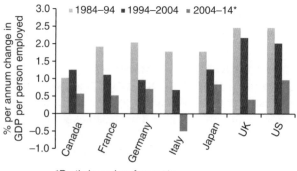

*Partly based on forecasts

Figure 3.2. Productivity slowdown across the West. *Source*: IMF World Economic Outlook.

This slowdown in productivity growth is the main reason for the disappointing economic performance of the Western economies in the New Normal. As the Nobel prize–winning economist Paul Krugman noted:

> Productivity isn't everything, but in the long run it is almost everything. A country's ability to improve its standard of living over time depends almost entirely on its ability to raise its output per worker.[17]

A similar growth and productivity slowdown occurred in the 1970s. And, as we saw in the previous chapter, there were other key parallels between that period and now: a big disruption to the financial system, a period of high and volatile energy prices and a big loss of confidence in government economic policies.

Why should these changes lead to a productivity slowdown? Productivity growth depends on businesses being able to extract more output from their resources of labour and capital each year. They can do this most easily when the economic climate is stable, demand is increasing steadily and predictably, and there is easy and cheap access to energy and finance. When economic conditions are volatile and uncertain, established patterns of demand have been disrupted and energy and finance become more costly or restricted, productivity growth is much harder to achieve. That was the experience of the Western economies in the 1970s and it underpins the growth slowdown we have seen since the financial crisis.

If we look back to the period before 2007, economic growth across the Western economies was underpinned by three tailwinds: easy money, cheap imports and confidence. All three have been undermined by the events we have seen in the global economy since the mid 2000s, including the financial crisis. These tailwinds have been replaced by three opposing headwinds: a constrained financial system, high and volatile energy prices, and prevalent uncertainty and lack of confidence. These are the forces which are shaping the current New Normal of disappointing growth in the major Western economies.

## The rise and fall of easy money

From the 1980s onwards, growth in the Western economies was supported by a deregulated financial system which provided consumers and businesses with relatively easy access to finance. Before the 1970s, the financial system in most Western economies was highly constrained, with controls on credit and bank lending, restricted competition and limits on the movement of capital across national borders. In the 1970s and 1980s, these restrictions on the financial sector were gradually removed – freeing up the availability of credit and allowing financial institutions to compete more freely. Movements of capital between countries were also encouraged by reductions in limits on international financial transfers and the deregulation of foreign exchange markets. In general terms, the financial system moved from a regime of detailed regulations and restrictions to a position where the main mechanism of control was the interest rate which national central banks set in the financial markets.

The first phase of this process of financial deregulation contributed to the strong boom of the late 1980s. To curb inflation and financial excesses, monetary policy was deployed – in the form of higher interest rates – to bring economies back under control. That, in turn, led to the recession of the early 1990s. But the downturn proved short lived for the major Western economies. Most of them moved back quite quickly onto the growth track that had been established in the 1980s.

In the 1990s the process of financial deregulation and liberalization continued, and developed a global dimension. China, India and other large emerging market economies started integrating into the world economic system – increasing the scope for flows of investment between the major Western economies and the developing world. The euro came into being as the single currency for the European Union, which facilitated financial flows between its member countries – with money moving to support investment in southern Europe and other peripheral European economies that had previously only had access to finance at much higher interest rates. Within the United States, the Clinton and Bush administrations encouraged the government-backed housing institutions, Fannie Mae and Freddie Mac, to increase their lending to low income households. In 1999, the United States also repealed the Glass–Steagall Act, which had been enacted in the 1930s to protect bank depositors by enforcing a separation between retail and investment banking.

The end product of all these measures, which freed up national and international movements of finance, was the global credit boom which started in the 1990s and gathered momentum in the 2000s.[18] Lending and the size of the banking system expanded rapidly, supported by the development of innovative new financial instruments, such as CDSs (credit default swaps) and CDOs (collateralized debt obligations). This surge in lending was encouraged and supported by interest rate reductions in the United States and other Western economies in response to the economic slowdown of the early 2000s. The US Federal Funds rate was held below 2% from the end of 2001 until the end of 2004. This pre-2007 credit boom was also underpinned by the belief in a new era of global economic stability which we discussed in Chapter 1. That, in turn, encouraged banks and investors – taking their cue from policymakers – to underplay financial risks.

This world of easy money supported a number of aspects of the pre-2007 growth phase in the West – strong growth of consumer spending and housing/construction booms in a number of economies. All this came to an abrupt end with the financial crisis. The freewheeling financial climate which sustained the pattern of growth pre-2007 is unlikely to return in the near term if at all. Banks which made big losses in the financial crisis are having to repair their balance sheets and are being much more cautious about the risks attached to new lending. In addition, new forms of banking regulation are being put in place to prevent a return to the behaviours which precipitated the financial crisis. These include the Dodd–Frank Wall Street Reform Act in the United States, which was passed into law in 2010, and the UK Financial Services Act of 2012, which implemented the proposals of the Independent Commission on Banking in the United Kingdom.

This change in the financial climate has removed one of the key drivers of economic growth in Western economies from the 1980s until 2007. The easy access to borrowing provided by a highly deregulated financial system has been replaced with a headwind of restricted access to finance and financial reregulation. Some economists see this change in the financial climate as the main factor accounting for disappointing economic growth since the financial crisis. This view has been promoted by the work of two US economists – Carmen Reinhart and Ken Rogoff – who analysed the experience of economies after financial crises over the last 800 years.[19] They find that economies suffering a financial crisis generally have a prolonged period of disappointing growth in its aftermath. This is often described as a process of deleveraging: large debts which were run up before the crisis are now being run down, and that is what is holding back growth.

However, there are other factors at work alongside this change in the financial climate. In addition to the disappearance of the world of easy money, other forces have also contributed to our current New Normal of disappointing economic growth. Western economies are no longer benefiting from two other growth tailwinds which supported economic progress before 2007: cheaper imports and confidence in the stability and predictability of the economy.

## The fall and rise of import costs

From the mid 1980s onwards, Western consumers benefited from a series of positive developments providing them with access to cheaper goods from the rest of the world. The first of these was the big drop in the oil price in the mid 1980s. The average price of crude oil – which had peaked at nearly

$37/barrel in 1980 and remained around $30/barrel until 1985 – fell in 1986 to below $15/barrel. If we take into account inflation, this was a 70% drop in the real price of oil compared with the early 1980s (see Figure 2.2 on page 24). This was a very big development in terms of the world economy. The cost of crude oil accounted for around 7% of world GDP in the early 1980s and this figure had dropped to around 2% by the late 1980s. This transfer of around 5% of world GDP to oil consumers at the expense of producers provided a major boost to consumer spending in most Western economies.

A second boost to Western consumers came from a reduction of trade barriers across the world economy in the first half of the 1990s. Negotiations started in the 1980s on three major liberalizing trade agreements which came into force in 1993, 1994 and 1995 respectively: the Single European Market; the North American Free Trade Agreement (between the United States, Canada and Mexico); and the Uruguay Round of the General Agreement on Tariffs and Trade (GATT). Trade agreements of this sort benefit consumers by providing them with access to cheaper goods from a wider range of producers. They also boost economic growth more generally by providing opportunities for efficient and competitive producers to expand into new markets.

A third benefit to the Western world came from the expansion of the world trading system in the 1990s and 2000s to include large emerging and developing economies like China, India and the former Soviet bloc countries. The ending of the Cold War and the collapse of the Soviet Union brought Russia and its satellite economies into the world economic system. But, just as important, it undermined the credibility associated with any alternative to the Western economic model, encouraging other emerging and developing economies to integrate into the market-oriented global economic system led by the

United States and Europe. In the late 1980s and early 1990s, both India and China embarked on a process of reform which opened up their economies to the world trading system. India was a founder member of the World Trade Organization when it was established in 1995 and China joined in 2001.

The expansion of the world trading system to Russia, China and India and other emerging market economies created new potential export opportunities for the established players in the world economic system – like the United Kingdom, United States and other European powers. But for Western economies, the most significant short-term effect was to provide consumers with access to much cheaper goods produced at a fraction of the labour costs paid by manufacturers based in Europe and North America. This 'China effect' created a period of flat or falling prices of manufactured goods across the Western world. Between the mid 1990s and mid 2000s, the prices of global manufactured goods rose by just 0.2% per annum in dollar terms and fell by 0.2% a year in euros. This contributed to low inflation in many Western economies in the late 1990s and early 2000s, including the United Kingdom, as Figure 3.3 shows.

Figure 3.3. Goods prices driving UK inflation.
*Source*: Office for National Statistics.

This benign global price trend did not last, however. As Figure 3.3 also shows, the period of flat or falling goods prices came to an end around 2004–5, when the impact of falling manufactured goods started to be offset by rising oil, food and commodity prices. This, too, reflected the impact of China, India and other large emerging market and developing economies – but in a different way. The strong growth of these economies over a prolonged period, and the development of their industries and middle-class consumers, is now putting upward pressure on inflation in the Western world through the effect on the price of energy, food and other commodities.

The IMF's index of oil and commodity prices shows a threefold rise between the early 2000s and early 2010s, as Figure 3.4 shows, with the financial crisis providing only a brief respite. At the time of writing (autumn 2013), the upward pressure has eased as growth has slowed across the world economy. But this respite may not last. Indeed, stronger global growth in 2014–15 could lead to another surge in energy and commodity prices, just as it did in 2003–5, 2006–8 and 2010.

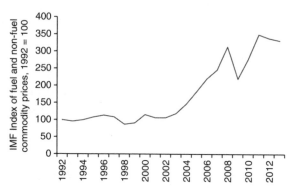

Figure 3.4. Commodity prices surged in 2000s.
*Source*: IMF World Economic Outlook.

Over a long enough period of time, the supply of commodities and energy should catch up with demand and help to stabilize and lower the prices for these vital natural resources. But the upward pressure from rising global demand in the opposite direction is powerful, suggesting that the current period of high and volatile energy, food and other commodity prices will be with us for a number of years yet. On the demand side, we now have over 7 billion people on our planet, with around 95% of them living in countries participating in the world trading system, through membership of the WTO. Also, as economists at HSBC have argued, the economies growing most rapidly at present – in Asia and other emerging regions – are at a more commodity-rich stage of their development.[20] Developments like oil shale and oil gas may help keep down energy costs at the margin, but they are working against very powerful forces on the demand side.

We should therefore expect the current phase of high and volatile energy and commodity prices to continue in the years ahead. In addition, improving economic prospects and wage growth in China and other 'low-cost' economies could start to feed through into rising prices of imported goods in the West. One way or another, the world of ever cheaper imports and the 'China effect' seems to have come to an end for the foreseeable future.

## Confidence gives way to uncertainty

The final ingredient contributing to the New Normal of disappointing growth in the major Western economies has been a loss of confidence among consumers and businesses in many countries. Before the financial crisis, confidence was fuelled by two main factors. The first was the experience of a long and sustained period of growth that started in the 1980s, gathered momentum in the 1990s and continued in the 2000s until the financial crisis hit in 2007–8. This long period of growth was also accompanied by improving employment prospects. Across the G7 economies, the unemployment rate fell back in the 1980s from the 1983 peak of over 8%, averaging 6.3% in the two decades before the financial crisis.

The second factor which fuelled confidence from the 1980s onwards was the perception that central banks and governments had reasserted control over their economies after the turbulence of the 1970s. As we have already observed, businesses, consumers and financial markets react badly to a situation where the public authorities do not appear to be in control of economic events. That feeds uncertainty and lack of confidence, holding back business investment and encouraging consumers to conserve cash rather than commit to major expenditures.

In the 1980s, governments and central banks in Western economies started to regain control after the financial volatility and high inflation of the 1970s. High interest rates and restrictions on the supply of money were used to get on top of inflation in the United Kingdom and the United States in the 1980s. Within Europe, countries linked their currencies to the low-inflation German Bundesbank as a mechanism for bringing inflation down. The success of the Bundesbank in resisting inflation in the 1970s and of the US Federal Reserve under Paul Volcker in restoring price stability in the 1980s greatly enhanced the credibility of independent central banks over this period. Though inflation picked up again in the late 1980s and early 1990s, monetary policy was quickly tightened to bring it back under control – even at the cost of a recession in the early 1990s. The credibility of central banks was reinforced further in the 1990s by the focus on targeting a low rate of inflation, which is a very clear and transparent basis for operating monetary policy. This was the basis of the policy regime introduced in the United Kingdom when the Bank of England was formally given independent control over interest rates in 1997.

At the same time, the 1980s and 1990s saw governments bringing their borrowing under control. Public sector deficits had ballooned in many countries in the wake of the oil price shocks of the 1970s and early 1980s. In response to these upward pressures on government borrowing and debt levels, there was a renewed emphasis in setting government spending and tax policies which would be sustainable in the medium term – rather than just using fiscal policy as a tactical tool to support growth in the short term. In the United Kingdom, the government adopted a Medium Term Financial Strategy from 1979 onwards aimed at both reducing the government deficit and controlling inflation. A similar policy approach was adopted in the United States and other European economies from the 1980s onwards, even if sometimes the reality deviated from the rhetoric. When the euro was established in 1999, rules were in place to contain excessive deficits, though they were not always enforced strictly. And in the 1990s and in the pre-crisis 2000s, healthy growth in other major Western economies – United States, United Kingdom and Canada – helped to keep tax revenues in line with rising government spending.

In the 1990s and early 2000s, when growth was threatened, Western governments and central banks seemed to be in a position to restore order. In response to both the late 1990s Asian crisis and the early 2000s economic downturn, cuts in interest rates appeared to be able to sustain growth in the face of these shocks. Governments also played a stabilizing role by maintaining the growth of public spending even though tax receipts had weakened with a softening economy. These actions added further to the confidence of financial markets, individuals and firms that whatever happened in the economy, central banks and governments could put the show back on the road.

This confidence, however, has been badly punctured by the financial crisis, and now needs to be restored. It is now clear that central banks cannot restore growth in the way we thought before the crisis. And increasingly indebted governments cannot do so either. At the same time, the experience of disappointing economic growth and prevailing uncertainty is a big dampener on confidence in households, private sector businesses and financial markets.

## The New Normal: tailwinds turn to headwinds

In a nutshell, the New Normal of disappointing economic growth in Western economies reflects the fact that three big tailwinds which supported growth from the 1980s onwards have disappeared and have been replaced by challenging headwinds. We are no longer in a world of easy access to finance, cheap imports and strong confidence. The stability of the financial system has been undermined and needs to be rebuilt. High and volatile energy, food and commodity prices are putting additional pressure on Western consumers. And the private sector and financial markets have lost confidence in the ability of the economic authorities to restore stability to the current economic order.

The tailwinds which supported growth before 2007 are not going to quickly resume. So we should expect the current period of disappointing economic performance to continue through the mid 2010s. Later, we will discuss how governments and central banks can restore control and how business should respond in this changed economic environment. But first, we will take a look at how different economies are faring in this New Normal world. Some are doing much better than others, and it is instructive to understand the forces determining who are the winners and losers in the new world economic order.

Chapter 4

# Winners and losers in the New Normal economy

Which countries are the winners and losers in the post-crisis New Normal economy? At first sight, the big winners appear to be emerging market and developing economies. Their growth has been resilient and they bounced back strongly since the financial crisis. The Western economies have shown much more disappointing performance – but there have been quite significant differences in growth among this group – particularly within Europe, as Figure 4.1 shows. North America and northern, central and eastern Europe have performed much better than southern Europe, where economies have generally seen declines in GDP since 2009, despite economic recovery elsewhere. It is clear that some Western economies are much better placed to prosper in the New Normal world than others.

This in turn raises two questions. First, can the emerging market and developing economies continue to perform as strongly as they have in recent years? Or is this another bubble that may burst in a year or two? The recent slowdown in some of the leading economies in this group – like China and India – has raised concerns about the durability of their growth. Second, why are some Western economies doing

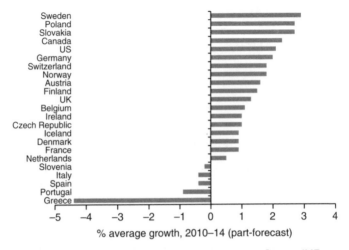

Figure 4.1. Winners and losers over the recovery. *Source*: IMF
World Economic Outlook, updated with PwC forecasts.

better than others? What are the characteristics which can
make for economic success in the West in the New Normal?

## The rise of Asia and other emerging economies

When I started studying economics at school in the 1970s,
most of the countries we currently describe as emerging
markets or developing economies were classified as part of
the 'Third World' or as Less Developed Countries (LDCs). The
bulk of Asia and Africa and many countries in Latin America
were seen as having very poor growth prospects, with very
little chance of coming close to the prosperity seen in the
'First World' – dominated by the United States, Western Europe and Japan. In the 1970s, the notion that China and India
could become economic superpowers would have seemed
far-fetched. The main challenge to Western domination of

the world economy seemed to be coming from the Soviet Union and its allies in Eastern Europe, which were trying to rival the Western world in economic development and technology by using state planning, rather than the market, to drive progress.

At the same time, there were a small number of Asian economies blazing a more successful economic trail: Hong Kong, Singapore, South Korea and Taiwan. These four 'tiger' economies began to achieve sustained high rates of growth which were the envy of other 'Third World' economies. Between 1960 and 1985, they grew by 6–7% a year on average, despite the economic turmoil in the global economy in the 1970s and early 1980s. Over a 25-year period, such sustained high rates of growth enabled these countries to increase the size of their economies around fivefold. And in the 1970s and 1980s a number of other East Asian economies began to follow their example and achieve similar results, including Malaysia, Thailand and Indonesia.

What was the secret of economic success that these high-performing Asian economies had discovered, that had eluded many other low-income economies? In 1993, the World Bank published a study of the experience of Hong Kong, Singapore, South Korea and Taiwan under the title: *The East Asian Economic Miracle*.[21] It identified five key ingredients of the economic success of the four 'tiger' economies and others following in their footsteps. First, they had pursued conservative macro-economic policies, keeping public sector deficits and inflation under control. Second, they had achieved high savings rates, which allowed a high capital investment rate to be sustained without depending on financial inflows from overseas, running the risk of a balance-of-payments crisis. Third, there was a strong emphasis on export-led growth, which had a dual benefit: tapping into the large potential of world markets and ensuring that businesses were internationally competitive and were not reliant on protected domestic markets. Fourth, these high-performing economies had invested in education and training so that they had a skilled workforce able to raise productivity and contribute to the success of the economy. Fifth, economic policies were pragmatic and adapted to changing circumstances. Some of these 'tiger' economies were more interventionist than others – South Korea and Singapore relied more heavily on state control of the economy than Hong Kong and Taiwan. But government interventions were judged on their economic success and adapted when they were not working.

In the 1990s, some much larger economies started to follow this economic model, after the collapse of the Soviet Union and the demise of its state-planning model of economic development. China and India both began to open up their economies to market forces and to integrate their economies into the world economic system. India was a founder member of the World Trade Organization in 1995 and China joined in 2001. Other former communist states like Vietnam followed the same market-oriented path. The three largest population economies in Asia – China, India and Indonesia – have increased their share of world GDP from less than 4% in 1990 to over 16% in 2013. The bulk of this increase has come from the rise in the share of the Chinese economy from less than 2% of world GDP in 1990 to over 12% now.

The increasing importance of these large Asian economies has shifted the balance of power in the world economy. As a result of their strong growth, the Asia–Pacific region has become the dominant force in the world economy. Taking all the economies in the region together – including Japan and Australia – the Asia–Pacific region now accounts for close to a third of world GDP (measured at market exchange rates).

During the 1990s and 2000s, Asia has overtaken both the United States and European Union in economic importance, as Figure 4.2 shows. This is a very significant shift from the situation in the 20th century when the United States and Europe dominated the world economy.

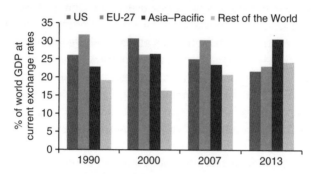

Figure 4.2. Asia–Pacific now the dominant region.
*Source*: IMF World Economic Outlook.

This shift in the centre of economic gravity towards the Asia–Pacific region is likely to continue rather than being reversed. About 60% of the world's population live in this region of the world economy and 40% of the people on our planet live in China, India and Indonesia. These economies are developing substantial middle-class populations and major world companies – like the Chinese mobile phone and communications company Hauwei and the Indian conglomerate Tata, which owns Jaguar Land Rover, Tetley and the former British Steel in the United Kingdom.

Over the past two decades, the Chinese economy grew at nearly 10% a year and it will not be able to match this growth rate in the future. Indeed, the Chinese government has set a target of 7.5% growth for the next five years. Since the early 1990s, India's economy has grown at close to 7% per annum, and the IMF and other forecasters expect economic growth to resume at around 6% following the recent slowdown. There is considerable potential for growth in these large Asian economies as average living standards are still very low by Western standards. At market exchange rates, average per capita income in India is just 3% of the level in the United States, 8% of US levels in Indonesia and 12% in China. There will inevitably be fluctuations in economic growth, as we have seen recently. But as long as these large Asian economies remain politically stable and can adapt their economies as living standards rise and new economic challenges present themselves, their importance in the world economy will continue to grow, with their share of world GDP rising to match more closely their share of global population.

The PwC's latest 'World in 2050' report[22] predicts that China will overtake the United States as the world's largest economy by 2030 and that India and Japan will then be the third and fourth largest economies in the world. Just as the 19th century was dominated by the European powers, and the 20th century was the 'American Century', the 21st century looks set to be shaped by the large Asian economies – notably China.

While the rise of Asia is at the heart of the growth of emerging market and developing economies, it is not the whole story. Two other ingredients have underpinned the strong growth of emerging market and developing economies we have seen since the 1990s. The first is the rise in energy and commodity prices as strong growth in the Asia–Pacific region has pushed up the demand for vital natural resources. This has benefited many economies which are producers of energy and basic commodities, particularly in Africa, which has been seeing its strongest growth phase since the 1970s. Russia and some economies in Latin America have also benefited from this resource-driven growth.

The second ingredient supporting the recent strong growth of the emerging and developing world is that there has not been a major political or financial crisis to disrupt progress, as we have seen in previous decades. In the 1970s and 1980s, Latin America suffered a lot of economic turbulence, with many countries running into problems of debt and high inflation. In the early 1990s, the break-up of the Soviet Union and the painful transition from state planning to a market economy created political and economic turmoil in Russia, Central Asia and Eastern Europe. And the late 1990s saw the Asian crisis temporarily disrupting the growth of economies in that region. Since then, while there have been some isolated problems in individual countries, we have not seen a major disruption to growth in a major region of the developing world – although it would be unwise to rule out the possibility altogether.

These two additional factors highlight where the risks may lie to growth in emerging and developing economies. Though my expectation is that we will continue to be in a world of relatively high energy, food and commodity prices for some time, the supply of these vital natural resources will eventually begin to respond to higher prices, as we have seen in the development of shale oil and gas in the United States. And high prices should also choke off demand as consumers and businesses adapt their behaviour. If energy and natural resource prices adjusted back to lower levels, this would create difficulties for economies excessively dependent on revenue from basic commodities. This risk to economic stability could be reduced if countries benefiting from high energy and commodity prices plough the revenues back into investment to diversify their economies and build up infrastructure. But past experience has showed that it is often easier for countries which are major producers of energy and other basic commodities to consume rather than invest the wealth that accrues when prices are high.

The other risk associated with emerging markets is a renewed bout of regional political or financial turbulence which disrupts the growth of a number of significant developing economies. The region where this would be most damaging would be in Asia, hence the critical importance of continuing stability in the large emerging market economies of that region, notably China and India. However, we could also see renewed economic difficulties in Latin America, and the combination of slow growth and high inflation in Brazil is starting to raise concerns about its economic prospects. Volatility is the price that investors often pay for high growth and high returns and that must always be a risk to be borne in mind when doing business in emerging market economies.

Despite these risks, however, the central forecast for the next five years or so is a continuation of the pattern of relatively strong growth in the emerging markets and developing economies – led by Asia. Figure 4.3 shows the IMF's latest

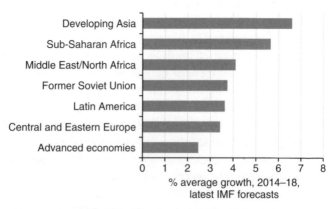

Figure 4.3. Growth projections to 2018.
*Source*: IMF World Economic Outlook.

forecasts which show Africa the second strongest growth area, reflecting the expectation of healthy demand for energy and commodities, coupled with high prices. But in general terms, the two-speed world economy which has been a feature since the financial crisis is projected to continue: healthy growth continuing in emerging markets and developing economies, coupled with subdued growth in the West.

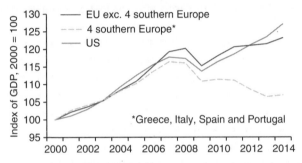

Figure 4.4. US and EU economic performance.
*Source*: IMF and author's calculations.

## Problems in Southern Europe

As we noted at the start of this chapter, however, some Western economies appear to be doing better than others in this New Normal world. The prevailing wisdom is that Europe is struggling while the United States is starting to shrug off the shackles of the financial crisis. But this is too simplistic. The weakness of in Europe is heavily concentrated in the four troubled economies of southern Europe, as Figure 4.4 shows. Excluding Greece, Italy, Portugal and Spain (which make up about 22% of European Union GDP), the growth profile of the European Union over the course of this century so far has been very similar to the United States. And the United States has had the advantage of stronger population growth, which boosts its growth figures by about 0.5% per annum relative to the European Union. So on a per capita basis, growth has been stronger in the bulk of the European Union than in the United States so far this century.

Why have these four southern European economies performed so badly in recent years? It is popular to blame the euro, and the fact that this has not allowed countries to devalue their way out of economic and financial problems. But it is not clear that exiting the euro would resolve the economic problems of southern Europe. It would simply result in a squeeze being imposed on these economies via a different route, with a sharp currency depreciation pushing up consumer prices and a crisis of confidence creating the need for a sharp rise in interest rates. This was the experience of Iceland, which faced the full force of the financial crisis in 2008–9 without the protection of the euro area. Interest rates rose to 17.5% before falling back to 3–5%. The value of the Icelandic krona halved in value and inflation hit a peak of over 18%. GDP in Iceland fell by 6–7% between 2008 and 2012 and is not projected to recover its 2008 value until 2016.

If there is a common theme to the situation facing Greece, Italy, Spain and Portugal it is that the pre-2007 world of easy money, cheap imports and strong confidence masked problems which were exposed in the full glare of the financial crisis. But these problems have a different complexion in each of the four troubled economies. In Greece and Portugal, the main issue was bad management of public finances before 2007. Both countries had high deficits before the financial crisis, and the 2008–9 recession made them worse, leading to the need for IMF support. Spending was not particularly high by European standards but tax receipts in both countries were low: around 40% of GDP compared with 45% across the euro area as a whole.

The problems in Italy and Spain were different. Spain experienced a private sector boom–bust cycle, driven by investment in property and construction. Strong private sector growth boosted public finances before the crisis, and Spain ran budget surpluses in 2005, 2006 and 2007. But when the property boom unwound, the damage to public finances was exposed: tax receipts collapsed while spending rose with the need to support unemployed workers and low income families. Recorded unemployment in Spain is over 26%, the second highest in Europe (after Greece).

The situation in Italy is more complex. Italy's ratio of public sector debt to GDP rose in the 1970s and 1980s and was already over 100% of GDP in the early 1990s. The criteria for joining the European single currency required high-deficit countries to manage their deficit ratios back to 60% of GDP but this was not seriously attempted by Italy, which had a series of weak governments through the 1990s and 2000s. This burden of past debt is the main problem for Italy's budget position. Without debt interest payments, spending and taxation were broadly in balance in the mid 2000s. The other problem Italy faced was a very low underlying growth rate, even before the crisis. As Figure 4.5 shows, Italian GDP showed no net GDP growth between 2000 and 2013–14, a very long period of stagnation.

There appear to be three main problems affecting the economic prospects of these southern European economies. First, with the exception of Spain, they appear to have poor growth fundamentals. Greece, Italy and Portugal have not increased their GDP over more than a decade since 2000, a worse performance than Japan's lost decade in the 1990s and early 2000s. In all three countries, GDP per head in 2013 was lower in real terms than in 2000, and in the case of Italy the decline has been over 6%. Second, the unwinding of

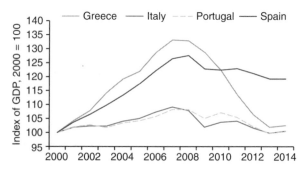

Figure 4.5. Southern Europe: mixed fortunes. *Source*: IMF.

boom–bust cycles in Spain and Greece has created the need for financial write-offs. In the case of Greece, this has involved a write-down of government debt; in Spain, there is a need to recognize large losses within the banks, particularly in relation to their property lending. Third, all four countries need to achieve a more sustainable position for their public finances, which requires a prolonged period in which government spending is constrained and/or taxes rise.

It is likely to be a long haul while these adjustments take place. And a successful transition to more growth-friendly policies in Greece, Italy, Portugal and Spain will require a high degree of political commitment over a period of five to ten years, not dissimilar from the transition which the UK economy made under Margaret Thatcher in the 1980s. It remains to be seen whether this can be achieved, particularly in Greece and Italy, where there is a long tradition of political instability.

## Northern Europe: Grounds for optimism

By contrast with southern Europe, the economies of northern and central Europe look better placed to achieve a recovery in growth in the New Normal world. There are three main reasons for being more optimistic about their prospects. First, Germany, Scandinavia and a number of other northern European economies have strong and competitive export-oriented industrial sectors which have been successful engines of economic growth for many decades. This success is built on developing strong positions in industries where technology and skills support high value added per person employed. Though the United Kingdom is very successful in some key sectors – like aerospace, pharmaceuticals and high-value-added engineering – it does not have such a broad manufacturing base as some other northern European economies. Manufacturing accounts for just over 10% of GDP in the British economy compared with over 20% in Germany, 19% in Austria and Finland and 16% in Sweden. However, the United Kingdom is a very successful exporter of services, second behind the United States in the value of services exports, and the largest exporter of services among the major economies on a per capita basis.[23]

Second, over the last three decades, most countries in northern Europe have undertaken labour market reforms aimed at increasing the flexibility of their economies. These reforms have encouraged the growth of service sector jobs and flexible employment patterns. They have also involved the use of so-called active labour market policies, which are government programmes targeted at raising the skill levels and employment prospects of disadvantaged groups in the labour force. These labour market policies have included an element of stick as well as carrot, with benefit entitlements being limited or reviewed if job seekers are not actively looking for work. These types of policies have been in place in Sweden since the 1960s, and have been introduced to other Scandinavian countries. The United Kingdom started a process of labour market reform aimed at promoting more wage and employment flexibility in the 1980s, and policies continued to evolve and develop in the 1990s and the 2000s. Germany embraced labour market reform under its social democrat chancellor Gerhard Schroder in the early 2000s in an attempt to address persistently high unemployment rates following unification. Germany's unemployment rate is now less than 7% of the labour force, compared with 11–12% a decade ago.

A third source of economic strength for Europe has been the expansion of the European Union and the Single European Market to incorporate the low-cost economies of central and eastern Europe. In 2004, ten countries joined the European Union, raising the number of member states from 15 to 25. The new members included seven former Soviet bloc economies – Poland, the Czech Republic, Slovakia, Hungary, Latvia, Lithuania and Estonia – as well as Slovenia, which was formerly part of Yugoslavia. Subsequently, in 2007, Bulgaria and Romania became members of the European Union and Croatia joined in 2013, taking the total membership to 28 nations.

Unlike the countries of southern Europe, which joined the European Union in the 1980s and became members of the euro, most of these central and eastern European economies did not share in the financial excesses of the late 1990s and 2000s. As a result, labour costs remain competitive, public finances are in reasonable shape and there have not been serious banking excesses. Only four of the ten Eastern bloc economies which have joined the EU since 2004 have joined the euro area. The larger economies – Poland, the Czech Republic, Hungary, Bulgaria and Romania – retain their own monetary policy independence and exchange rate flexibility.

Within Europe, economic prospects seem to be divided by a new Maginot Line[24] which runs from the low countries of the Benelux to the eastern Mediterranean. While there are

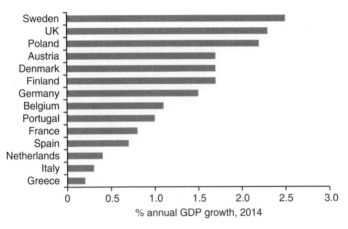

Figure 4.6. European growth forecasts for 2014. *Source*:
OECD, updated with PwC projections for larger economies.

some exceptions among smaller economies, Figure 4.6 shows
that economic growth prospects are much more positive to
the north and east of this line, underpinned by Germany and
other economies with stronger economic fundamentals. To
the south and west, economic conditions are more problem-
atic. This view of Europe places France in the same camp as the
southern European economies, which may seem harsh. Yet
the French economy is struggling to grow. It may have some
highly competitive and innovative businesses. But France has
not embarked on a serious programme of labour market and
welfare reform like other northern European economies, and
it has a high level of government spending and taxation, even
by European standards. In 2013, public expenditure is projected by the OECD to be 57.1% of GDP compared with a euro
area average of 49.7% and 45.5% in Germany.

Alongside the United States, there are grounds for optimism that the more flexible and competitive economies in
northern, central and eastern Europe – including the United

Kingdom – can support a recovery in growth in the West. But to underpin this economic turnaround, governments need to wrest back control of their economies and restore confidence in economic and financial stability. How they might do this is the subject of the next chapter.

Chapter 5

# Recovering control: how should policymakers respond?

The picture described in earlier chapters is of a world of relative stability and strong confidence across the Western world which was disrupted by the financial crisis in 2008–9. The disappearance of the pre-2007 world of easy money, cheap imports and strong underlying confidence has left the major Western economies in a New Normal of weak growth and economic volatility.

The initial response of policymakers to the financial crisis was to pull out all the stops – cutting interest rates, making injections of money through quantitative easing and allowing public sector deficits to rise. These policies were successful in preventing a financial meltdown. But they are not necessarily the right policies to support a return to stronger growth over the long term. Businesses and consumers know that when the government is running a large deficit and its debt is building up rapidly, there will need to be a future correction to restore financial discipline, either by bringing spending down or pushing taxes up. Until it is clear what the nature and scale of that adjustment will be, the private sector will be naturally cautious about future investment and spending commitments.

Similarly, the very low interest rates which were used to support economies in the depths of the crisis are still in place. Central banks have accumulated large quantities of government debt and other financial assets. Uncertainty about how these very expansionary monetary policies will be unwound adds to the lack of confidence in future prospects. Prolonged low interest rates may also be helping to support underperforming businesses by easing the pressure on them to restructure and adapt to the New Normal world.

Western governments and central banks therefore need to move out of their 2008–9 fire-fighting mode and start to set out a policy agenda which will command more confidence in the longer-term stability of their economies. In my view there are four key elements to such a policy programme. The first is to reform and restructure government so its spending commitments are sustainable and compatible with the reduced New Normal growth of economies. Second, central banks need to develop credible exit plans to achieve a gradual shift away from the emergency monetary policy settings put in place in response to the crisis. Third, policymakers should implement a comprehensive agenda of supply-side reforms which are aimed at supporting growth and employment in private businesses, which in turn underpin the process of wealth creation. And fourth, we need a new wave of free trade agreements aimed at expanding market opportunities and boosting business confidence, just as we saw in the early 1990s.

## Public sector restructuring and reform

Across the Western world, public spending as a share of GDP has risen since the financial crisis. As Figure 5.1 shows, government spending averaged about 36% of GDP in the United

States before the crisis and around 47% in the euro area with the United Kingdom somewhere between these extremes. These figures rose sharply in 2008–9 to hit nearly 43% in the United States and over 50% in the euro area and the United Kingdom. This was not mainly due to a conscious decision to increase public spending – it predominantly reflects the declines in GDP during the recession of 2008–9 and previously planned rises in expenditure. But the impact of recession on tax receipts, coupled with slow growth over the recovery, means that public spending plans need to be reined back considerably if government deficits are to be brought back to sustainable levels.

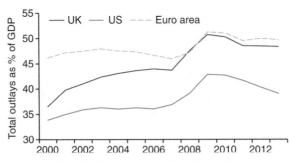

Figure 5.1. Government spending in the
Western economies. *Source*: OECD.

It is tempting to see this as a short-term challenge requiring a few years' restraint of public spending and then getting back to normal once the deficit is brought down. But that would be a mistake for two reasons. First, there is a danger that policymakers will base their view of what can be afforded by the public sector on the 'old normal' world of stronger growth pre-2007. So an adjustment is needed to weaker economic growth in the New Normal as the tax revenue available to fund spending is growing more slowly than we would have expected before the crisis. Second, there is a wide range of structural pressures pushing up public spending in Western economies – ageing populations creating rising pension payments and social care costs, higher expectations of health and education service provision and the rising cost of new medical treatments and technology. To offset these pressures in a low-growth environment, Western governments need to have a long-term plan for ensuring that the demands on the public sector do not outpace the ability of the economy to fund them.

There is no single obvious and easy solution. In mature Western economies, the public sector is a large and complex legacy business, which has been accumulating and developing its activities since the beginning of the 20th century. As a result, the share of GDP devoted to government spending has typically ranged from around a third in the lowest-spending countries (e.g. Switzerland and United States) to over 50% in the high spenders (France and Scandinavia). In an increasingly globalized world economy, raising taxes is not a solution either. Higher taxes on the income of companies and individuals threaten to undermine competitiveness, and encourage economic activity to relocate. And higher taxes on consumers and firms will intensify the squeeze that they are already feeling as a result of the aftermath of the financial crisis as well as rising energy and food prices.

To adapt and reform government to meet the challenges of the 21st century, we need to consider more radical options. First, government may need to withdraw from the provision of some public services altogether, leaving these to be provided by the private sector. Second, benefit and public service entitlements which are available for the better-off members of society may need to be withdrawn so that public funds can be focused on more-needy individuals. Third, governments should be striving to improve the delivery model for public services, so that they are provided much more efficiently and effectively to those who need them.

This is potentially a massive agenda for public sector re-structuring and reform, particularly for countries which are still projected to have large deficits five to six years after the onset of the financial crisis. That includes the United Kingdom and United States as well as southern European countries, as Figure 5.2 shows. But the benefit of embracing reform in the public sector is that government is freed up to deploy resources to invest for the future – in skills, technology and infrastructure. Governments which are encumbered by high debts and deficits do not have the flexibility to do this, as Britain found out to its peril in the late 1970s and early 1980s.

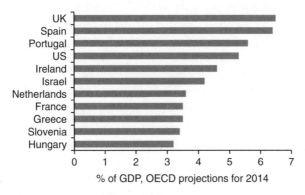

% of GDP, OECD projections for 2014

Figure 5.2. Public deficits: selected OECD economies. *Source*: OECD Economic Outlook, June 2014. Note: countries shown have projected deficit of over 3% of GDP in 2014.

## Planning for the monetary policy exit

Very low interest rates and injections of money through quantitative easing (QE) have been important parts of the stimulus provided to Western economies to support growth since the crisis. But there are signs that these policies are becoming less effective and may even become counterproductive. We saw in Chapter 1 that more recent injections of monetary stimulus appeared disappointing in terms of their impact on growth in the United States and United Kingdom. There are also concerns about the distortions in the economy these highly stimulatory policies may create if they continue.

One potential distortion is by inflating the prices of more risky financial assets and physical assets, like equities and housing, creating an artificial asset market bubble. Another problem is that borrowers may be encouraged to gear up by a prolonged period of low interest rates, making the transition to higher rates much more difficult without delivering an unpleasant shock to the economy. A third distortion is the depressing impact on savings income. Well-off savers may be able to ride out a period of low interest rates by dipping into their capital or finding alternative investments. But people with low levels of saving and low incomes are much more vulnerable to a prolonged period of low interest rates eroding their income, causing them to cut back on spending. They may be penalized doubly if inflation continues to run at a relatively high level, as it has done in the United Kingdom since the financial crisis.

For these reasons, I have always been in favour of making a gradual exit from the loose monetary policies put in place in 2009. In the United Kingdom, there was an opportunity to start that process in late 2010 and early 2011, but the majority of the Bank of England MPC did not support my case then. There may be another opportunity arising in 2014–15 if the world economy picks up as forecast and the growth of some of the major Western economies starts to look stronger, helping to reduce unemployment.

If interest rates do start to rise gradually in the major Western economies, they will still be low by historical standards. The 0.25–0.5% interest rates we now currently have across the United States, United Kingdom and euro area are much lower than we saw in the Great Depression when official interest rates did not fall below 2% in the United Kingdom (in 1932). In the United States they fell further – but more slowly – to 1.5% by 1934, dropping to 1% in 1937.

The concern that central banks clearly have about making the first upward move in interest rates is that it will lead to a belief that a sharp correction is on the way, and that this will create a negative shock to confidence. That makes it all the more important that central banks effect a well-communicated and gradual exit from current very loose monetary policies, and reassure the public and businesses clearly about their intentions. Unfortunately, the policies of the US Federal Reserve and the Bank of England are going in the opposite direction. They are committing to keeping official interest rates at very low levels, while the unemployment rate remains higher than a specific level (6.5% in the United States and 7% in the United Kingdom) and inflation is still under reasonable control. The risk attached to this approach to policy is that by keeping borrowing costs low for longer, a sharper upward correction is eventually needed – delivering precisely the shock to confidence which policymakers are currently trying to avoid! If unemployment lags behind other indicators of economic recovery – as we have seen in the past – this risk of a delayed sharper monetary policy response increases further.

While there is uncertainty about the exit strategy for monetary policy, it is likely to act as a dampener on long-term investment decisions. Businesses and consumers should draw confidence from the notion that central banks have a well-worked-out exit strategy. While this strategy is unclear, there is likely to heightened uncertainty about the future macro-economic climate, holding back investment.

## Supply-side measures to support growth

The third way in which policymakers can support growth in the Western economies is through a renewed programme of supply-side reforms to support the growth of private sector businesses. It is the market system which underpins private sector activity and, as Adam Smith pointed out, the 'invisible hand' of the market operates to ensure resources are allocated efficiently across the economy. To achieve this, regulatory barriers and tax distortions should be kept to a minimum, and government interventions in the private sector should be targeted primarily to remedy obvious market failures. Because supply-side policies are enabling rather than directive, their impact on economic growth is not as immediate as policies which focus on injecting demand into the economy. The private sector will take time to respond to new incentives and opportunities. However, this also means that a supply-side growth strategy should produce a more sustainable growth benefit, in contrast to demand management policies which are best suited to achieve a short-term boost to growth, for example, to help lift an economy out of a deep recession.

The prime objective of supply-side policies is to help businesses by enabling them to operate more efficiently and effectively. But there is a potential boost to demand from these policies as well, in two main ways. First, creating a more internationally competitive economy can boost exports and encourage inward investment. Improvements in the business climate should help firms become more competitive so they are better placed to develop new business opportunities in overseas markets. Similarly, supply-side reforms aimed at creating a more business-friendly climate should help attract internationally mobile foreign investment. Second, a well-communicated and coherent strategy of supply-side reform can boost business confidence and support investment by creating a more positive view of medium-term growth prospects. In the current environment, where business confidence is weak and many companies appear to be conserving cash for this reason, this could be especially useful. However, to generate this confidence boost and to influence investment decisions, it is important that policy measures are sustainable over the long-term. Short-term measures will not necessarily have the same impact.

Supply-side reform played an important role in underpinning the recovery of the UK economy in the 1980s. Nationalization and state intervention in industry gave way to privatization and deregulation of markets. The tax system was reformed and marginal tax rates were brought down. Labour market policies changed dramatically, with the protection afforded to unions reduced, and a renewed emphasis on labour market flexibility. But policies driven by a strong free market ideology also had to be adapted over time to take into account practical realities. In the late 1980s and 1990s, there was recognition that while the state needed to pull back, inadequate investment in infrastructure, education and research could harm the economy. And labour market policies needed to strike a balance between flexibility and deregulation and remedying problems facing specific groups who lacked the skills and motivation to compete for available jobs. Employment and training programmes were developed to help long-term unemployed workers become more competitive in the labour market, and this helped to underpin the reduction in the UK unemployment from over 10% of the labour force in the mid 1980s to around 5% in the late 1990s and 2000s (prior to the financial crisis).

From the 1980s onwards, four key themes underpinned supply-side policies in the United Kingdom and other Western economies. These principles can help to inform a new wave of supply-side reform to invigorate growth in the aftermath of the financial crisis.

### (i) Market liberalization and efficient regulation

Market disciplines generally create more efficient outcomes and support economic growth. Resources in the economy are allocated more efficiently, rather than being hoarded in inefficient sectors. Businesses are encouraged to become more responsive to changing patterns of demand and the development of new technology. And in markets open to international trade, domestic producers will face an additional spur to efficiency from foreign competitors, who may be able to produce goods and services more efficiently, more cheaply or to a better quality standard.

However, not all markets can operate successfully in a purely competitive environment. Natural monopoly, public goods and other market characteristics mean that some form of regulatory market intervention is needed. There may also be non-economic reasons for regulation of business activity – such as the need to protect the environment, reduce inequality of income or protect health and safety. In these situations, what we should be looking for is efficient regulation, which allows markets to operate as efficiently as possible, minimizing the burdens on business and barriers to growth. Designing systems of efficient regulation is a major challenge in a modern economy open to international competition, and it is essential to regularly review regulatory frameworks to ensure they are achieving the objectives which they were originally set up to achieve.

## (ii) Tax reform

Taxes can have a significant impact on economic growth and business competitiveness. For example, the UK government currently raises close to 40% of GDP in taxes and the tax burden is likely to remain around this level into the future. However, the way in which tax revenue is raised can distort economic activity. In the light of experience and economic analysis, a number of principles have come to inform the design of efficient tax systems. First, tax rates need to be kept as low as possible, to avoid distortions to incentives. This implies that policymakers should seek to define a broad tax base and avoid a large number of exemptions. Second, tax rates should be kept as low as possible on the creation of wealth – income generation, savings and investment and corporate activity. Taxes on expenditure and accumulated wealth are less distortionary, and taxes on socially and environmentally damaging activities (e.g. smoking, alcohol consumption and burning fossil fuels) can be beneficial for society. Third, efficient tax systems should treat very similar goods, services and economic activities equally. Otherwise, there will be distortions to spending and economic activity which are motivated purely by the structure of the tax system resulting in economic inefficiency.

## (iii) Labour market flexibility and efficiency

The performance of the labour market is a key issue for the efficient functioning of the economy, as our analysis above showed. An established body of economic analysis and the experience of the United Kingdom and other major economies in dealing with labour market inflexibilities and imbalances since the 1970s have taught some important lessons about how labour market policies should develop in mature Western economies. In summary, there are three main conclusions which flow from a vast body of analysis which has been carried out on this subject.[25–27]

First, the efficient operation of labour markets is supported by a relatively liberal and deregulated environment. Regulations which give generous benefits and rights to existing employees or impose large non-wage costs on employers will discourage hiring of new workers and contribute to high medium-term levels of unemployment. Second, employment regulations which impose reasonable standards in terms of minimum wages and other employer obligations are not intrinsically harmful to employment, but the imposition of these regulations and standards need to be sensitive to changing labour market conditions. At times of high unemployment and weaker labour demand, new labour regulations could be particularly damaging. Third, the benefit system, employment taxes and regulation and the provision of skills by the education and training system are crucial to the operation of the labour market. Hence, government can use the policies proactively to address specific labour market problems. This view underpins the notion of 'active' labour market policies which were first deployed in Scandinavia but have become more commonplace in the United Kingdom and other northern European economies in recent years.

(iv) *Infrastructure investment, education and research*

The efficient operation of the private sector in market economies depends on the public sector investing in a number of key strategic activities to provide the infrastructure which supports economic growth and development – transport networks, the education system and basic research. Basic research may not be such an important issue for countries at a relatively low level of standard living – where they can deploy a strategy of 'catch-up' with more advanced economies in science and technology. But Western economies are not generally in that position. The more successful economies in the West – the United States, and the stronger economies of northern Europe including the United Kingdom and Germany – have drawn strong economic benefits from being world leaders in key areas of scientific research and applying the insights to the development of new and improved products.

## Opening up the world trading system

The final way in which policymakers can support growth in the current economic environment is through opening up trading opportunities between the major economies in the world. One of the most important insights in economics has been the theory of comparative advantage advanced by David Ricardo in the nineteenth century.[28] The idea behind Ricardo's theory is that while one country might be more efficient at producing everything than another country, both countries would benefit from trading with each other and the result would be that each country would specialize in the industry where they had the best relative (or comparative) advantage. This idea was a powerful boost to the free trade movement in the 19th century and a serious blow to the earlier mercantilist idea that industries needed to be protected with barriers to trade and high import duties.

More modern economic theories of international trade have stressed other advantages from trade. These include the consumer benefits of access to a variety of goods and the opportunity for producers to take advantage of economies of scale. That, in turn, can make businesses more prepared to bear the risks of investment in new technologies and innovation. The link between trading opportunities and economic growth is therefore well established in economic theory and practice. As we saw in Chapter 3, a number of agreements designed to open up European, North American and global markets to international trade in the first half of the 1990s helped support the long growth phase which continued until the financial crisis.

Discussions are now underway on a number of new agreements which will help further reduce the barriers to trade across the global economy. The United States and a number of countries in the Pacific region started negotiations in 2010 on a Trans-Pacific Partnership free trade agreement. In the summer of 2013, Japan joined the talks, adding significance to the potential agreement. More recently, the United States and the European Union have started discussions on a Transatlantic Trade and Investment Partnership (TTIP). The European Union is also in discussions with Japan and Canada on free trade or more liberal trade agreements, as well as with a number of other countries around the world.

In the 1930s, a wave of protectionism deepened the Great Depression and added to the difficulties of the world's major economies. As the world economy has recovered from the recent financial crisis, this new round of agreements has the potential to go in the opposite direction – unlocking growth potential in world markets for many businesses. Over and above that, if world leaders are able to rise above national protectionist sentiments and allow their consumers to access goods and services from around the world more freely, that could also provide a major confidence boost to growth prospects.

## Can policymakers deliver?

On all the four agenda items above, there are big challenges for policymakers. Reforming the public sector and restraining government spending raises political sensitivities. Central bankers are clearly nervous about raising interest rates in case they undermine recovery. Supply-side reforms may involve challenging vested interests or removing regulatory protections – such as changes to the planning system in the United Kingdom. And there is also opposition to a new round of free trade agreements – for example from unions representing workers who feel their jobs may be threatened by overseas competition. Indeed, international policy coordination of any sort faces major challenges in terms of reaching agreement and ensuring that the policies agreed are properly implemented.

In the 1980s, the changes in policy which helped kick-start a new growth wave were led by politicians who had clear ideas about the economic and political changes they wanted to achieve. In the United Kingdom and the United States, Margaret Thatcher and Ronald Reagan championed market disciplines, control of public spending and tax reform. Helmut Kohl and François Mitterrand championed the integration of Europe which led to the Single European Market and a single European currency. Western leaders came together to encourage the process of reform in the Soviet bloc in the late 1980s which ultimately led to the break-up of the Soviet Union and the integration of its economies into the global economic system.

The vision that underpinned these responses seems lacking in the current political debate in the West. The emphasis still seems to be mainly on dealing with the legacy of the financial crisis rather than trying to create a future vision for the Western world. We will return to this issue in Chapter 7 in discussing the prospects for a new more positive growth phase in Western economies when the headwinds holding back growth in the New Normal world have eased. But before considering that, the next chapter considers how businesses – particularly those based in the major Western economies – should be responding to the current economic climate, and the opportunities and challenges ahead.

Chapter 6

# Business success in
# the New Normal

How should businesses respond to the New Normal economic climate which we have experienced since the financial crisis? The natural response to the onset of the crisis was to shock many businesses into survival mode. So the emphasis was on conserving cash, reducing costs, avoiding any non-essential expenditure and postponing investment. The fact that the major Western economies have experienced relatively sluggish growth since the crisis has reinforced and sustained these cautious behaviours in many companies. Investment remains very subdued relative to pre-crisis levels as a result and many businesses appear to be conserving their financial resources, rather than committing to major capital expenditure. This is reflected in very subdued capital spending across the major Western economies, as Figure 6.1 shows.

The analysis presented so far in this book would appear to support this view. If growth is much weaker and different in character going forward, surely it is right for businesses to take a cautious view and hunker down. However, there are two potential flaws with this strategy. First, business is a competitive activity. If your business is not seeking out new opportunities and trying to identify new sources of profit and

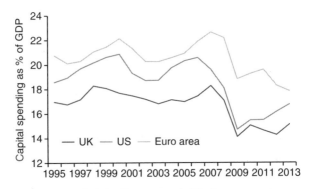

Figure 6.1. Subdued investment in Western economies.
*Source*: IMF World Economic Outlook.

growth in a more competitive environment, it is quite possible that your competitors are stealing a march on you. And
in the highly globalized economy we now inhabit, many actu-
al or potential competitors could be based in Asia and other
emerging market economies which are performing more
strongly.

We can see these competitive challenges emerging in the
1970s and early 1980s, the last time the Western economies
went through a slowdown comparable with our post-crisis experience. Despite the unfavourable general economic climate,
some of the giants of the modern computing world came into
being at that time. Paul Allen and Bill Gates founded Micro-
soft in 1975 and Apple Computers was established in 1976.
These businesses made great progress in developing the
emerging personal computer and software markets and, by
the 1980s, were challenging established computer giants like
IBM. During the 1970s and early 1980s, Japanese motor manufacturers made major incursions into Western car markets
and by the mid 1980s Nissan was building its first major car
manufacturing plant in the west, in Sunderland in northeast

England. South Korea established its shipbuilding industry in the declining and depressed markets of the 1970s and 1980s, growing its market share from virtually zero to 25% between the early 1970s and late 1980s.[29]

A second reason why caution and conservatism may not be a sound strategy in the New Normal world is that this is a time of significant structural change in the economy. Markets that supported strong growth in the pre-2007 world are now less dynamic. Companies that do not adapt themselves to the changes which are taking place in the economy – by seeking out new sources of growth – risk being stranded with under-performing assets and businesses, which are not well suited to the post-crisis world.

One of the big sources of structural change in the Western world is the weaker trend growth of consumer spending. The pre-2007 drivers of growth – easy money, cheap imports and confidence – supported strong growth in consumers' expenditure in Western economies and encouraged a wave of investment in property and construction. Across the OECD economies, real consumer spending grew by nearly 3% per annum for the two decades 1987–2007, and in the United States and the UK growth was over 3% a year. The trend in the growth of consumer spending since the crisis has been very different. As Figure 6.2 shows the real level of consumer spending is still not expected to recover to 2007 levels by 2014 in the United Kingdom and the euro area. And the consumer recovery has been relatively muted in the United States compared with the pre-crisis trend.

Yet despite these unfavourable macroeconomic trends, there are still areas of business opportunity and significant growth in Western consumer markets. These are being driven by a range of factors, including technology (e.g. online re-tailing, tablet computers), emerging social trends (Twitter,

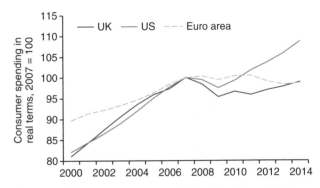

Figure 6.2. Weaker consumer trend in the New Normal. *Source*: OECD Economic Outlook. Note: 2013 and 2014 are forecasts.

Facebook, etc.), new products and services, and lower-cost versions of existing products and services. And while Western consumer markets are currently subdued, North America and the European Union still jointly account for around 55% of total world consumer spending – a much bigger share than their combined share of world GDP.

## Rebalancing to manufacturing?

If hunkering down is not the right strategy, where might companies look for new business opportunities and growth? It is tempting to look for a new mega-trend, or set of mega-trends, which will replace the growth forces we left behind in 2007. One popular view in some Western economies – including the United Kingdom – is that a rebalancing of the economy towards manufacturing can help replace the strong drivers which supported growth before the crisis. Germany, which has benefited over many decades from having a strong manufacturing economy and has performed relatively well since the financial crisis, is often cited as an example which other Western economies should follow. But Germany has the advantage of a much larger manufacturing base than almost any other Western economy. Manufacturing industry accounts for over 20% of German GDP, compared with 13% in the United States, 11% in France and just over 10% in the United Kingdom. In Britain, manufacturers now account for just 8% of total employment, compared with around 30% in the late 1970s.

I am a big supporter of manufacturing industry. As a member of the Bank of England Monetary Policy Committee from 2006 to 2011, I visited many British manufacturing companies – particularly smaller and medium-sized companies. But the characteristics of these businesses and the challenges they face do not suggest that a manufacturing renaissance is on the cards in the United Kingdom or in the majority of other Western economies.

Competitive advantage in manufacturing is a long-term game for high-income Western economies. Manufacturers based in the West do not have the obvious advantage of low labour costs. Success has to be built up over time – by the deployment of high levels of skill, technical know-how, innovation, design, supply chains, brand reputation, sales and distribution networks, etc. These conditions for success cannot simply be switched on because we have suffered a financial crisis or allowed our exchange rate to fall. And the manufacturing markets where Western economies might want to increase their share are also being targeted aggressively by businesses based in Asia and other emerging regions, which have the added advantage of relatively low labour costs and may also benefit from more supportive government policies. China is already the world's largest producer of solar panels and is now targeting other high-technology markets, like aerospace and electric cars.

Manufacturers with substantial operations in Western economies are therefore often facing a challenge of defending existing market positions, keeping themselves ahead of the competition through a focus on innovation, quality and design and on maintaining a highly skilled workforce. Where there could be more potential for manufacturing growth is from smaller entrepreneurial businesses, exploiting new ideas and technologies developed in university science departments and laboratories. But it will take time for such businesses to establish themselves and grow to any significant size. These business start-ups may also need some specific support – in the form of tax incentives, management advice or preferential access to finance – to help them in the early phases of development. Historically, the United States has had a better record than Europe in developing these entrepreneurial university-based businesses, partly because their universities are more dependent on private sector funding, which has fostered stronger relationships with the business community.

It is not a surprise, therefore, that manufacturing industry has not been the powerful engine that has pulled the Western

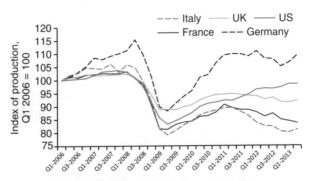

Figure 6.3. Manufacturing output in Europe and the United States. *Source*: OECD.

economies out of the 2008–9 recession. As Figure 6.3 shows, with the exception of Germany, manufacturing output in the leading Western economies is still below its level in 2006. While manufacturing industry in the West can and should contribute to the recovery, we are not likely to see a dramatic industrial renaissance lifting us out of the New Normal of disappointing growth.

So where do the growth opportunities lie for businesses in the New Normal world? Rather than look towards a new mega-trend, a tide which will float all ships, businesses need to look at ways in which they can reposition themselves within the markets in which they already operate or capitalize better on capabilities that they already have. With more limited growth now available from a favourable macroeconomic environment, businesses need to look more to exploiting opportunities created by emerging trends or competitive advantages that they can identify through their detailed understanding of the markets in which they operate.

There are four broad areas where companies might look to develop strategies which might help ensure business success in the post-crisis, low-growth, economic environment in Western markets.

## Opportunities in Asia and emerging markets

First, businesses which have traditionally served Western economies need to think about ways in which they can take advantage of the strong growth in Asia and emerging markets. This is already an important component of the strategy for many Western companies, particularly manufacturers who can develop their exports to fast-growing markets. But services businesses have a lot of export potential too. We are accustomed to thinking of exports as a physical activity where something is shipped to one part of the world economy to another. But from an economic standpoint, an export is simply a transaction where someone overseas pays you for what you do. That overseas customer could be buying widgets. But they could also be commissioning a consultancy report or requesting legal advice. They could be a tourist, or a student visiting your country to study. These are all export activities, which are recorded as trade in services rather than goods.

Trade in services is currently the Cinderella on the world trade scene – the global value of trade in goods is four to five times higher than services in value terms. However, a recent analysis by PwC economists showed that the value of services imported by emerging market and developing economies exceeded the G7 total for the first time in 2010.[30] Transport and travel, financial and business services – such as legal advice, accountancy and consultancy – are all major growth areas for services exports to emerging/developing economies. And this is an area where the UK economy in particular does relatively well, as we noted in the previous chapter. The United Kingdom exports significantly more services as a share of GDP than other major economies, as Figure 6.4 shows.

## Harnessing technology and innovation

Another powerful source of growth and competitive advantage in the New Normal world is the application of new technology and the process of innovation. We have already noted that there is little sign of slackening in technological change across the world economy. In addition to the development of information and communications technology linked to the

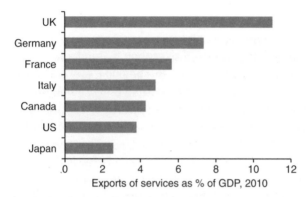

Figure 6.4. United Kingdom leads on services export contribution.
*Source*: OECD Statistics on International Trade in Services.

Internet and the growth of mobile devices, significant advances are being made in the development of new materials, genetics and energy technologies. Moreover, if the number of patent applications is a guide, the pace of technological development is quickening. In 1990, there were just under 1 million patent applications worldwide. The number had risen to 1.37 million in 2000 and reached 2.14 million in 2011. Just as Asia is becoming more important to the world economy more generally, it is becoming a more important region for innovation and technology, with 54% of all world patent applications originating in Asia in 2011, compared with just 35% in 1990.[31]

Some companies can exploit the potential of new technology and innovation because that is the nature of their business. They focus specifically on the development and application of new ideas and techniques. These 'technology sector' businesses include biotechnology companies and developers of computer software and hardware. But a much wider range of businesses are users of technology, seeking to deploy it to achieve competitive advantage, whether as a retailer developing their online presence or as a manufacturer trying to keep ahead of competitors with the use of new materials, designs and processes.

There are a number of ways in which technology shapes the business environment, creating both new opportunities and competitive threats and challenges. First, it can be a driver of cost reduction and efficiency. This is a very traditional role which technology has played going back to the earliest days of the industrial revolution, such as the invention of the Spinning Jenny and the Spinning Mule, which revolutionized the production of cotton and other fabric materials. Second, technology supports the introduction and evolution of a vast array of new products and services, again as we have seen throughout history, with the development of the steam engine, motor cars, powered flight and a whole range of electrical and electronic goods.

Another role that technology plays is in breaking down barriers between markets. Improvements in transport systems have reduced the importance of geography in separating markets. And we now see the Internet and other developments in mobile communications technology playing a similar role – increasing the transparency of prices, reducing distribution costs and broadening consumer access to a much wider range of goods and services. In particular, the Internet has transformed the market for travel, providing a platform for the growth of low-cost airlines and allowing consumers to bundle or unbundle their holiday plans in the way it suits them, rather than in a way dictated by a package-holiday provider.

A final role which technology plays is through shaping the way in which our society and economy is organized. Public transport systems have had a major influence on the development of cities and the patterns of urban life. And we now see developments in social media changing the way in which we interact and communicate in society, as well as dramatically increasing the flow of information outside the control of established media organizations.

## Getting the business basics right

For all these reasons, the ability to harness new technology for competitive advantage and respond to the challenges it is creating for established ways of doing business will be a key driver of business success in the New Normal world. But in addition, businesses will need to become much smarter and more flexible in terms of the way they respond to their customers and their competitors. In the pre-2007 world, when Western businesses were being supported by the strong tailwinds of easy money, cheap imports and confidence, the rising tide of strong economic growth helped to keep businesses afloat and sustained their profits – even if they were not strong performers within their sector or industry. The current low-growth environment is much more demanding. Businesses which do not have sound fundamentals will increasingly struggle and may not survive.

What are the business basics which need to be mastered to succeed in the current more demanding business environment? I would highlight three in particular. First, an ability to understand and adapt to changes in markets since the financial crisis. This applies in particular to consumer-facing businesses which are now having to acclimatize to much lower growth. Second, a strong focus on delivering value to customers and being prepared to adapt and change the customer proposition if that is not the case. The customer is king in the New Normal economy. Companies which perform better than average in a low-growth environment are those which can convince their customers they are getting good value from the goods and services that they buy. Good value does not necessarily mean being the cheapest – it means ensuring the combination of price, quality and the experience of the product/service delivers customer satisfaction. The third element of business basics is having a flexible and adaptable business model, which can respond to changing customer requirements and adjust costs to more modest growth of revenues. Businesses which lack operational and cost flexibility, and have high fixed costs and overheads, are unlikely to be able to achieve this.

A good example of how this has played out in practice is the experience of UK retailers since the financial crisis. Given the subdued growth of UK consumer spending shown in Figure 6.2, it is not surprising that there have been some casualties in the retail sector. In the five-year-period 2008–12, over 200 retail businesses failed, affecting a total of nearly 20,000 retail outlets and over 180,000 jobs.[32] Retailers selling durable goods, like furniture, carpets and electrical appliances, have suffered particularly as consumers deferred purchases in the recession. There have also been significant challenges for retailers whose markets have been heavily penetrated by online sellers, such as retailers of electrical and electronic goods, music and videos. But other retailers have prospered and grown. The more successful businesses are those which responded more quickly to the challenges of the downturn in 2008–9, sought to reduce fixed costs and adapt to changing patterns of consumer spending. In particular, the more successful retailers have developed the potential of selling online alongside their traditional store offering, providing consumers with a range of different channels to make purchases. The value of online retailing in the United Kingdom has grown by over 20% per annum since 2007, with the share of retail sales online increasing from 4% of total to over 10%.[33]

## Meeting new energy and environmental challenges

The final area of business opportunity in the current New Normal economic climate lies in adjusting to the combination of energy and environmental challenges the major Western economies are now facing. As we noted in Chapter 3, we are now in a world of high and volatile energy prices. As long as energy demand continues to be supported by strong growth in Asia and other emerging markets, and the supply of energy lags behind demand, this situation is likely to persist. For many businesses, this is simply seen as an extra cost burden to be managed, absorbed by profit margins or passed onto customers. But there are areas of opportunity in the energy world too, particularly in the context of the need for economies to move to a lower-carbon and more energy-efficient economic model, if we are to contain the rise in greenhouse gas emissions and limit climate change and global warming.

There are three main areas of potential growth and business development created by this situation. The first is the challenge of developing new sources of energy to meet demand. A lot of recent attention has been focused on the potential of a technique called fracking to develop sources of shale gas and shale oil. But this is just one example of how new techniques and approaches can be used to bring on stream new sources of energy. A second challenge is to make progress in the transition to a low-carbon economy by maximizing the potential of renewable and other sources of low-carbon energy. World consumption of solar power stood at just 1 TWh in 2000 and was still below 7 TWh in 2007, yet

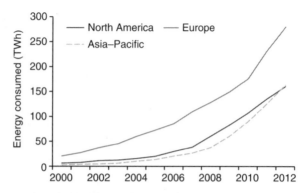

Figure 6.5. Growth of solar and wind power. *Source*:
BP Statistical Review of World Energy, 2013.

reached 93 TWh in 2012. Solar energy consumption across the world has tripled in the past two years alone. There is a similar story for wind power, where consumption had risen to nearly 18 times its level at the turn of the century by 2012.[34] These are explosive rates of growth, which are occurring in all the three main regions of the world: North America, Europe and the Asia–Pacific region, as Figure 6.5 shows.

The contribution of these renewable sources to meeting total world energy demand still looks small – less than 2% of world energy consumption is met by renewable sources. But the incremental impact is much greater, with 13% of additional energy demand being met by increased production of renewables in 2012. In addition, there are other potential sources of low-carbon energy waiting to be developed – such as carbon capture and storage systems applied to power stations which burn conventional fossil fuels, as well as third- and fourth-generation biofuels – using algae, modified organisms or advanced biochemical methods of production.

A third area of business opportunity created by current energy and environmental challenges is exploiting the potential for greater energy efficiency. In a world of high and volatile energy prices, efficiency becomes a very important tool through which businesses and consumers can manage their costs and reduce risk. Energy efficiency can also play a significant contribution in the transition to a more sustainable economy, alongside expanding the available sources of low-carbon energy. A whole range of tools are available to support and encourage energy efficiency, including home insulation, smart meters, smarter appliances, eco-labelling, and the use of lighter materials in vehicles and aircraft. In each of these areas, there is a wide range of business opportunities to be developed.

## Understanding and exploiting new drivers of growth

This is clearly not an exhaustive list of how businesses can succeed in the New Normal economy. If there is a common theme in the agenda outlined above, it is in focusing on the micro drivers of growth – within individual markets and sectors – rather than looking for a new set of macro trends to replace the tailwinds which supported growth before 2007. The benefit to businesses of doing this is twofold. First, it can help support growth and profitability in a more difficult economic climate. But, in addition, businesses which seek out and develop new opportunities in the current economic situation are likely to be better positioned if we do make the transition to a better growth phase in Western economies in the late 2010s or 2020s. Like the Silicon Valley pioneers who established their businesses in the 1970s and benefited from the boom in the information technology and communications industries in the 1980s and 1990s, those who seek out new opportunities in a difficult economic climate are likely to be better placed when the new drivers of growth are stronger and clearer.

But how likely is it that the major Western economies will make a transition to a new growth phase in the foreseeable future, after the disappointing economic performance of recent years? That is the subject of the next chapter.

# Chapter 7

# Towards a new growth phase?

I s the recent New Normal of disappointing growth a permanent downward shift in economic prospects for the major Western economies? This view is certainly gaining ground, just as pessimism about growth and employment prospects in the major Western economies gained ground in the 1970s and early 1980s.

A recent example is the book by Stephen King, Chief Economist at HSBC in London. You only need to read the title to get the main message: *When the Money Runs Out: The End of Western Affluence*. The introduction to the book sums up King's dystopian[35] view as follows:

> With ten years already of weaker than expected growth, the claims we all make on increasingly limited resources simply do not add up. Tensions that already exist between the world's creditor and debtor nations thanks to, for example, the Greek financial crisis will only escalate in the years ahead. Those who want their money back will only push harder to be repaid. Those who have borrowed will increasingly struggle to keep their creditors happy. Strains between the generations will surely increase. With the baby boomers heading into retirement fully expecting a combination of reasonable

living standards and generous medical support, the young may struggle to make ends meet, faced with a mixture of higher education costs, more expensive housing and higher indebtedness. And, after thirty years of dramatic increases in income inequality in the Western world, economic stagnation threatens to destabilise an already tense relationship between rich and poor.[36]

## Lessons from Japan

King and others who take this pessimistic view draw significant parallels between the situation now facing the major Western economies and Japan in the 1990s. In the early 1990s, Japanese economic growth seemed to hit a brick wall after four decades of strong expansion. As Figure 7.1 shows, after growing at 9–10% in the 1950s and 1960s and 4–5% in the 1970s and 1980s, the Japanese economy slowed down to a growth rate of about 1% per annum in the early 1990s. The trigger for this slowdown appeared to be a financial crisis in which banks had overextended themselves, particularly in terms of lending to the property sector. This was followed by a period in which the Japanese government allowed the budget deficit to expand and sought to support growth with fiscal stimulus, while the central bank cut interest rates to extremely low levels and periodically embarked on QE-style injections of money.

This all sounds very similar to the recent experience of Western economies, and there are certainly some parallels between the Japanese situation in the 1990s and the position in the West now. But there are important differences too. First, it took the Japanese authorities the best part of a decade to properly recognize and start to deal with the problems of non-performing loans and lack of capital in the banking

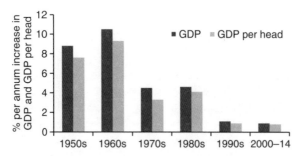

Figure 7.1. Japan's falling growth rate.
*Source*: Maddison Growth Project and IMF.

system. Even though these problems in the financial system emerged in the early 1990s, they only started to be addressed in Japan towards the end of the decade, when the Asian financial crisis triggered a new wave of bank failures and it was clear that the economy was locked into a prolonged period of deflation. By leaving the challenges facing the financial system unresolved for so long, there was a much more prolonged negative impact on the ability of banks to make new lending and on confidence more generally.

By contrast, the United Kingdom and United States moved quickly to recapitalize their banks in the immediate aftermath of the 2008–9 financial crisis. On the continent of Europe, there has been much slower progress in addressing problems in the banking system and this is contributing to the length and depth of the euro crisis. Even so, within the euro area, action is now being taken to shore up the banking system– including proposals to establish a European Banking Union overseen by the ECB. So even in the euro area, policy action has been quicker than the response of the Japanese authorities following their financial crisis in the early 1990s.

The second difference between the position of the West now and Japan in the 1990s is that Western economies moved much more quickly to relax monetary policy after the global financial crisis. Indeed, in the late 1980s and early 1990s, Japanese official interest rates were initially raised, from 3–4% in 1988–89 to over 8% in early 1991. Reductions in interest rates were then gradual, with the official interest rate dropping to around 3% in 1993 and to 2% by 1995. It was only in late 1995 and 1996 when the Japanese authorities were seeking to combat the negative impact on their economy of a very strong yen, that official interest rates were moved to the near-zero levels we now see in the major Western economies. Quantitative easing was not deployed in Japan at all in the 1990s to reinforce the effects of monetary stimulus. It was only in 2001 that the Bank of Japan rather half-heartedly started to deploy QE as a policy tool and not surprisingly – over ten years on from the start of the problems in the financial sector – it had little effect.

A third feature distinguishing Japan's experience from the current position of Western economies is the structural challenges facing the Japanese economy in the 1990s. A large part of Japan's economic slowdown in the 1990s can be attributed to the failure to achieve stronger productivity and employment growth in the services sector. Japan's recovery after World War II was driven by very impressive progress in manufacturing productivity. Japanese manufacturers set out initially to emulate the model of high-productivity mass production which they saw underpinning the success of the United States and leading European economies. They then set out to improve on that model.[37] This provided for very rapid manufacturing productivity growth as the Japanese producers of cars and electrical and electronic goods caught up with Western levels. But to go beyond that, Japan needed to push the technology and productivity frontier beyond what was being achieved in the United States and Europe. This was a much harder task, requiring high levels of research and development. It was not surprising that the achievable growth rate in manufacturing industry slowed down as a result.

In the services sector, however, Japan was not emulating Western approaches. Productivity in services was generally low and in key sectors, like retailing, overstaffing was rife. Consumers bore the costs of low services productivity by paying relatively high prices for retail goods and consumer services. Unlike manufacturing, the services sector was not subject to the pressures of international competition, so there was less urgency to raise productivity to match Western standards. Vested interests blocked reform which might have opened up services industries to inward investment by US- or European-owned firms. So economy-wide productivity, which is dominated by the performance of the services sector, remains low by Western standards, with recent estimates showing Japanese hourly productivity still about 15% below the United Kingdom and 30–35% below Germany, France and the United States.[38] Female participation in the workforce in Japan is also low by Western standards, which limits the supply of labour to support the growth of the services sector economy.[39]

Another structural ingredient in Japan's economic slowdown was demographics. As we saw from the figures presented at the beginning of Chapter 3, Japan now has a declining population whereas many Western economies – including the United States, United Kingdom and Canada – are expected to continue to see healthy population and employment growth. Once growth figures are adjusted for population changes, by expressing them on a per-capita basis, Japan's economic performance looks much more respectable compared with other Western economies. As Eamonn Fingleton points out, since 1989 the difference between US and Japanese growth

99

performance is much lower on a per-capita basis than in absolute terms. US GDP per-capita growth since 1989 has been 1.4%, whereas Japan's has been 0.9%.[40] The same point is clear from Figure 7.2, which shows the rise in living standards in G7 economies since 2000. Japan is in the middle of the pack, alongside the United States and Canada. Perhaps the surprising performer in this league table is the UK economy, which comes second behind Germany. And the poor performance of Italy, where living standards are 6–7% down on 2000 levels, is equally striking.

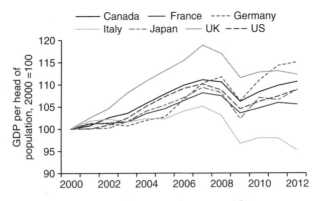

Figure 7.2. Relative performance of G7 economies since 2000. *Source*: IMF.

So to predict that the Western world as a whole is bound to follow Japan's path would be too pessimistic. The leading Western economies have dealt more quickly with their financial sector problems and responded much more swiftly than Japan adjusting monetary policy. The more successful Western economies also have a track record of stronger service sector productivity and employment performance, as well as more favourable demographic trends.

## Lessons from the 1980s

A more encouraging precedent for the West is provided by the turnaround which a number of economies achieved in the 1980s, after the slow growth and turbulence of the 1970s. Though it didn't appear likely at the time, 1982 was a watershed year for the major Western economies. As we saw in Chapter 2, a number of major Western economies started to make the transition to stronger growth in the early 1980s. And yet the economic background did not look at all promising. Unemployment was at post-war record levels in most economies. Inflation was only just coming down after the rapid price rises of the 1970s. And there was political and social unrest in many countries. In the United Kingdom, serious riots took place in a number of major cities in 1981: London (Brixton), Birmingham (Handsworth), Leeds (Chapeltown) and Liverpool (Toxteth). At the time, this appeared very much like the dystopia which Stephen King is warning us about – a period of disappointing economic growth causing societies and nations to turn on each other.

On the international stage, 1982 did not look encouraging either. The early 1980s seemed to be the darkest days of the Cold War. Yuri Andropov was appointed leader of the Soviet Union. He was a former leader of the KGB associated with suppressing the 1956 Hungarian Revolution and the 1968 Prague Spring, as well as cracking down on Russian dissidents. After he was appointed, Ronald Reagan described the Soviet Union as the 'Evil Empire'. And protesters gathered on Greenham Common in England to prevent the deployment of Cruise missiles, a new generation of nuclear weapons targeted on the Soviet Union.

But despite this inauspicious backdrop, instead of turning on each other, the major countries of the world began to look for positive and constructive solutions to their economic problems, both internally and externally. In the United States and the United Kingdom, as we have already noted, supply-side policies started to invigorate economic performance. As governments and central banks started to get on top of the main economic problem of the 1970s – inflation – public and business confidence began to return. New service industries started to emerge to support growth and employment, to replace traditional industrial sectors where the West was in decline, such as steel, shipbuilding and coal mining. And despite warnings that cuts in budget deficits would deepen recession, economic growth recovered.

Within Europe a new agenda for economic integration emerged in the 1980s, based on breaking down internal barriers to trade and maintaining economic and financial stability along the lines followed by the German Bundesbank after World War II. On the broader international stage, Western leaders forged a new relationship with Yuri Andropov's successor, Mikhail Gorbachev.[41] And the process of reform and change which then followed in the former Soviet Union paved the way for the opening up of the world economy in the 1990s and the new era of globalization which has prevailed since the mid 1990s.

So while we should not underplay the turmoil created by the recent financial crisis, it is also important to view our recent difficulties in the context of many positive developments which have taken place since that turning point in the early 1980s. Living standards have risen significantly across all the major Western economies. In the case of the United Kingdom, GDP per head is now around double the level achieved in the early 1980s. We have seen massive developments in information and communications technology based on personal computers and the development of the Internet. And businesses and consumers have the benefits of access to a highly integrated world economy, in which the bulk of the world's population – living in Asia and other emerging economies – is much better placed to share in future prosperity.

## The growth transition facing the West

Which scenario is the most likely for the Western economies in the aftermath of the global financial crisis: prolonged stagnation, on Japanese lines, or a growth renaissance such as we saw in the 1980s? If we look back to the way in which Western economies made the shift to a new growth phase in the 1980s and 1990s, after the doldrums of the 1970s, three key ingredients underpinned the transition. The first was the emergence of a supportive financial regime, with deregulation and liberalization of the financial sector allowing consumers and businesses to access credit more freely. The second ingredient was a return to more stable economic policies – grounded in a commitment to keeping down inflation and limiting government spending and borrowing. The third ingredient was the adjustment within businesses to find new sources of growth. As we noted in Chapter 5, this can be helped and encouraged by supportive supply-side policies, including opening up international markets to create more business opportunities and increase competition.

In the case of Japan, these adjustments have not taken place or are still incomplete, which accounts for the difficulties its economy has encountered in returning to sustained growth. The question for the Western economies now is how far advanced are we are along the transition path of necessary adjustments in the financial system, government economic policy and in terms of business restructuring?

It is clear that the transition is underway, but in no sense is it properly complete across the Western world. Within the financial system, there are two main elements to the adjustment process. The first is repairing the balance sheets of banks and other financial institutions which got into difficulty in the crisis and, in some cases, needed official support. In the United States, the federal government sold its stake in Citigroup at the end of 2010 and it has largely wound down its Troubled Asset Relief Program (TARP), which was used to ease the burden of bad loans made by banks. In the United Kingdom, the two state-owned banks – Royal Bank of Scotland and Lloyds Banking Group – have returned to profit and the government has started to sell shares in Lloyds back to the market. Within the euro area, however, there is still a legacy of unresolved banking problems, particularly in southern Europe. Over the summer of 2013, Spain and Italy both reported rises of 20% or more in the number of non-performing loans. And high unemployment and falling property prices in these economies are likely to aggravate this problem.

The second aspect to the adjustment in the financial system is the establishment of a new regulatory regime which seeks to increase resilience by requiring banks to hold larger buffers of capital and liquidity. In the United States, this has been implemented through the Dodd–Frank Act, which was signed into law in July 2010. But elsewhere the transition to a new regulatory structure is still work in progress. Between 2013 and 2018 the new Basel III requirements setting higher levels of capital and liquidity for major banks will be gradually brought in. The UK Financial Services (Banking Reform) Bill – which aims to implement the recommendations of the Independent Commission on Banking – is still making its way through parliament. And proposals within the European Union to establish a Banking Union – which aims to bring bank supervision and regulation in the euro area under a common European structure – have still not been formally agreed.

In addition to these changes in the financial system, Western economies need to shift away from the emergency policy settings put in place to combat the crisis and return to more stable and sustainable economic policies. This is another case of 'work in progress'. Deficits are gradually being reduced, with the OECD projecting that the combined borrowing of its member economies will have more than halved in the first five years of recovery, falling from 8.2% of GDP in 2009 to a forecast 3.8% in 2014. Here, the euro area collectively has made most progress, with a projected deficit of just 2.5% of GDP in 2014, less than half of the expected deficits in the United States (5.3%) and United Kingdom (6.5%).[42] In southern Europe, deficits are also coming down: in Greece from 15.6% of GDP in 2009 to a projected 3.5% in 2014 and from 11.2% and 10.2% of GDP respectively in Spain and Portugal to 6.4% and 5.6%.

However, the process of monetary policy normalization has not yet started, with interest rates still at rock-bottom levels and the US Federal Reserve still debating its policy of tapering quantitative easing. So while the private sector and financial markets can take some comfort from falling levels of government borrowing, it is still not yet clear if central banks can manage a smooth transition away from the current exceptionally low level of interest rates. Already, markets are starting to anticipate a gradual upward move in official interest rates in the United Kingdom and United States. Longer-term interest rates have also started to move upwards, with US ten-year bond yields rising from below 2% at the start of 2013 to nearly 3% at the time of writing. There has also been a degree of scepticism in financial markets around the new Bank of England policy of 'forward guidance' which aims to commit to continuing low UK interest rates until 2016.

Markets are currently pricing in the first rise in rates in 2015, and some commentators, myself included, believe it could come earlier than that.

The final element of the growth transition for Western economies hinges on how businesses adjust and respond to find new sources of opportunity. Here, it is clear that some countries are better positioned than others to tap into the new growth trends we identified in the previous chapter. In general, the economies of North America and northern and central Europe appear best placed. Their flexible labour market structures, strong culture of innovation and enterprise, established positions in high-tech, high-value-added manufacturing, and well-developed service sector economies should serve them in good stead, even in a world economy which is becoming increasingly dominated by the Asia–Pacific region.

## Growth prospects for Western economies

How will all these forces play out in the West, as we move through the second decade of the 21st century? This will depend on how quickly and fundamentally economies make the financial, economic policy and business transition described earlier in this chapter.

In the 1980s, the United Kingdom and the United States led the transition to a new growth phase for the Western economies. Short-term economic forecasts suggest that this could be the case in the mid 2010s, with 2014 forecasts for the United States, the United Kingdom and Canada above 2% and other G7 economies projected to grow more slowly.[43] However, it is important to note that these three Anglo-Saxon economies also benefit from stronger population growth, as we noted in Chapter 3. The differences between major economies in per-capita GDP growth are much narrower.

In Chapter 3, we also noted that productivity growth rates in Western economies had slowed progressively since the 1980s. Part of this slowdown reflects longer-term structural changes. As economies become more service-sector oriented, it is harder to achieve the rapid productivity growth that is available in manufacturing industry. This tendency, first pointed out by the economist William Baumol in the 1960s, is likely to mean that Western economies will not recover to the strong growth rates we saw from the early 1980s until 2007. The fact that this growth phase was supported by the strong tailwinds of easy money, cheap imports and confidence should also lead us to expect that we will not return to the pre-2007 growth trends, even if Western economies pick up from the current subdued New Normal growth pattern.

A good rule for economists is 'Don't forecast anything, especially the future'. So it might be unwise to predict how this transition might unfold. But you would be disappointed if I did not give my view. So that is the subject of the final chapter of this book.

Chapter 8

# Adapting to survive and thrive

The financial crisis and the disappointing growth which has followed it have fuelled fatalism about economic prospects for the major Western economies. One common pessimistic view is that without the rapid expansion of lending and the financial system that we saw before the crisis, there is no prospect of returning to healthy and sustained growth rates. Another is that the emergence of China and the Asia–Pacific region has fundamentally undermined the growth model of the Western economies. A third strand of pessimism relates to the role of the public sector. Plans and commitments for government provision of pensions, benefits and public services which were made in better economic times are no longer sustainable. A long and painful battle to contain government spending and adjust public expectations lies ahead; this may not be successful and it could also seriously dampen growth prospects.

The pessimistic case sees these as insuperable obstacles to a resumption of sustained growth in Western economies. A more optimistic view is that to survive and thrive in the post-crisis world, countries need to adapt their economic models to changed circumstances. If policymakers, businesses and individuals do not recognize this, then the economic outlook may indeed be bleak. The more successful economies will be those which seek to adapt and change to be equipped to prosper in the new post-crisis world.

We cannot make a definitive forecast of who will ultimately succeed in making this transition. The process of adjustment is underway, in the financial sector, in terms of economic policy, and in the business world. But it is far from complete. The success of Western economies will depend on their ability to see through this adjustment process and find new sources of growth to support a future phase of rising prosperity. Looking back to the forces and drivers which sustained growth before 2007 is unlikely to provide a good guide to future prospects. So we should not expect growth to be supported by the same financial behaviours which prevailed in the 1990s and 2000s. We need an approach from banks and other financial institutions which has learned from past mistakes and is adapted to the changes in financial regulation which are now coming into force.

Similarly, business needs to find new sources of growth to replace the strong impetus that was provided by the financial sector and Western consumer spending before the financial crisis. As we discussed in Chapter 6, this means looking to tap alternative sources of growth: the dynamism of the Asia–Pacific region and other emerging markets; new innovations and developments in technology; changes in business models and patterns of consumer behaviour; and the potential of new sources of energy and more environmentally sustainable patterns of economic activity. As we discussed in Chapter 5, supportive supply-side policies can help to encourage the development and growth of new businesses to offset the impact of the inevitable restructuring as economies adjust.

In the public sector, a similar process of adjustment is needed and, as we noted in Chapter 7, there has already been some progress in reducing deficits in the United Kingdom, the United States and the euro area even in the disappointing New Normal growth climate. There is no single-bullet solution to readjusting and reforming the public sector. Ring fencing and protecting specific categories of spending could be counterproductive. Essentially, governments need to review all areas of public spending in the search for efficiency improvements, new approaches to service delivery and to identify areas where the private sector can play a larger role and relieve the burden on the state.

Finally, just as in the 1980s, these adjustments are likely to be easier to achieve if we can maintain and reinforce the relatively free and open world trading environment which was established before the financial crisis. Opening up the world trading system is sometimes likened to riding a bicycle – if you are not moving forward quickly enough, there is a danger of falling over! So, just as in the 1990s, progress in the current round of regional and global trade discussions would provide important impetus to a recovery in Western growth prospects.

The turnaround made by the West in the 1980s shows that mature economies can regenerate and restructure themselves and make the transition to a new growth phase. But there is an important difference between then and now. The major Western economies are no longer able to call the shots on the international stage, and these economies will not necessarily set the rules of the global economic game in the way that they have done in the past. The balance of economic power is shifting away from the West and towards the Asia–Pacific region and other emerging economies.

The United Kingdom, the United States and other Western economies can no longer take growth for granted. Economic success will need to be earned by productive and flexible businesses which can generate value-added in highly competitive world markets. The policies which will foster national economic growth will be those that provide the stability, support and confidence which will help these businesses to thrive and adapt to changing market conditions. This, in turn, requires a willingness to accept and embrace structural change.

These underlying realities have been masked in recent years by the highly stimulatory policies pursued in the aftermath of the financial crisis. It has appeared that economic growth depended on the amount of monetary and fiscal fuel which has been injected into the fire. That fuel has now lost its potency. Looking ahead, Western economies need to rely on more fundamental drivers of economic growth – innovation and enterprise as well as the skills, productivity and flexibility of the labour force.

In the West, the future still lies in our own hands. With the right economic policies, and a willingness of the business and financial world to adjust to a changed economic climate, growth can recover to a stronger and more sustained pattern than we are seeing in the current New Normal. But the transition is not likely to be politically easy – governments need to be prepared to stay the course and defend unpopular decisions, as we saw in the 1980s. Nor would I expect a future rising tide of growth to float all ships. Western economic success is most likely to be focused around the two historic poles of growth: northern Europe, where modern industrial development started in the 18th and 19th centuries, and the United States, which established itself as a major economic power in the 19th and 20th centuries.

The world is divided into two types of people: natural optimists and natural pessimists. Faced with the same situation where the outcome is finely balanced, the optimists will see the glass as half full whereas the pessimists see it as half empty. I am a 'glass half full' person. And I am optimistic that we can return to more positive growth trends in the leading Western economies. But it will take time. The mid 2010s are likely to be a transitional period, with continuing ups and downs. And some economies will find it harder than others to get back on a sustained growth track.

As Mark Twain commented in response to inaccurate newspaper articles on his demise: 'Reports of my death are an exaggeration'. The economies of the West – which have powered the world economy since the 18th century – are not terminally doomed to stagnation. They are capable of regeneration. But we need to be prepared to adapt to survive and thrive.

# Endnotes

1.  See OECD Interim Economic Assessment, September 2013 (http://
www.oecd.org/newsroom/advanced-economies-growing-again-b
ut-some-emerging-economies-slowing.htm). The G7 economies are
the US, Japan, Germany, France, the UK, Italy and Canada.

2.  The IMF's measure of world economic growth at PPP exchange
rates averaged over 5% in the four years 2004 to 2007.

3.  The previous weakest years of postwar growth for the global
economy were 1.1% in 1982, 1.3% in 1991, 1.5% in 1975 and 1.7% in 1998,
based on data compiled by the late Angus Maddison of the University of Groningen (http://www.ggdc.net/maddison/oriindex.htm ).

4.  Speech by Gordon Brown, Chancellor of the Exchequer to the UK
House of Commons. *Hansard* HC Deb 17 March 2004, vol. 419, cc301–
36.

5.  As measured by the Retail Prices Index, UK consumer prices rose
on average by 2.7% in the fifteen years 1993–2007. The lowest figure
for a comparable period before inflation took off in the 1970s was
3.1% (1953–67).

6.  The proceeds and conclusions of this conference are written up
in the *Bank of England Quarterly Bulletin* 2008Q2, pp. 174–83.

7.  In the *Star Trek* episode 'Devil in the Dark' Mr Spock says, 'There
is no life... at least, no life as we know it.' In a subsequent episode
'Errand of Mercy' he has the line 'Fascinating... Not life as we know it
at all.' These quotes were used to form the basis of lines attributed
to Mr Spock in the 1987 pop song 'Star Trekkin': 'It's life, Jim, but not
as we know it...'

8.  In the four years of global recovery so far, 2010–13, the latest IMF
estimate of average annual world GDP growth is 3.8%. *Source*: IMF
World Economic Outlook, October 2013.

9. The OECD economies comprise the richer economies of the world. There are 34 countries mainly comprising North America, Europe and the more advanced Asia–Pacific economies: Japan, South Korea, Australia and New Zealand.

10. See http://blogs.ft.com/gavyndavies/2013/07/16/no-tapering-ye t-for-global-central-banks/

11. 'Lessons from history', speech by Ben Bernanke at the 43rd Alexander Hamilton Awards Dinner, 8 April 2010 (http://www.federalres erve.gov/newsevents/speech/bernanke20100408a.htm).

12. Speech at the Economic Club of New York, December 2012 (http:// econclubny.com/events/Transcript_MervynKing2012.pdf).

13. Milton Friedman and Anna Schwartz. 1963. *A Monetary History of the United States, 1867–1960.* Princeton University Press.

14. Barry Eichengreen and Douglas Irwin. The protectionist temptation: lessons from the Great Recession for today (http://www.voxe u.org/article/protectionist-temptation-lessons-great-depression-to day).

15. Using data from the latest IMF *World Economic Outlook*, G7 labour force growth (numbers employed + numbers unemployed) is projected to be 0.5% per annum 2004–14, in line with population growth at the same rate.

16. For a detailed discussion of the case for pessimism about innovation and technology, see *The Economist*, 12 January 2013, Has the ideas machine broken down?

17. Paul Krugman. 1990. *The Age of Diminished Expectations: US Economic Policy in the 1990s.* MIT Press.

18. For a more detailed analysis, see Michael Hume and Andrew Sentance. The global credit boom: challenges for macroeconomics and policy. Bank of England Monetary Policy Committee Discussion Paper 27 (http://www.bankofengland.co.uk/research/Pages/extern almpcpapers/discussionpaper27.aspx).

19. Carmen M. Reinhart and Kenneth Rogoff. 2011. *This Time Is Different: Eight Centuries of Financial Folly.* Princeton University Press.

20. Paul Bloxham, Andrew Keen and Luke Hartigan. Commodities and the global economy: are current high prices the New Normal? (http://www.panasiacorp.com.au/_content/documents/656.pdf).

21. World Bank. 1993. *The East Asian Miracle: Economic Growth and Public Policy.* New York: Oxford University Press.

22. PricewaterhouseCoopers LLP. 2013. *The World in 2050* (January).

23. TheCityUK Independent Economists' Group. 2012. Trade and infrastructure as drivers of global growth: what are the opportunities for the UK? (November). UK exports of services in 2010 were $239bn, behind the US at $545bn and ahead of Germany at $238bn. On a per-capita basis UK exports are $3,854 per head of population compared with $2,902 for Germany and US services exports of $1,763 per head.

24. The Maginot Line was a series of fortifications and defences constructed along the border between France and Germany between World Wars I and II.

25. Richard Layard. 1986. *How to Beat Unemployment.* Oxford University Press.

26. Richard Layard, Stephen Nickell and Richard Jackman. 2005. *Unemployment: Macroeconomic Performance and the Labour Market.* Oxford University Press.

27. Organisation for Economic Co-operation and Development. 1994. *The OECD Jobs Study.* OECD.

28. David Ricardo was a British economist who lived from 1772 to 1823. In his 1817 book, *On the Principles of Political Economy and Taxation,* he first formalized the theory of comparative advantage which had earlier been referred to by Adam Smith in his book *The Wealth of Nations* (1776) but not set out so clearly.

29. L. Bruno and S. Tenold. 2011. The basis for South Korea's ascent in the shipbuilding industry, 1970–1990. *The Mariner's Mirror* Vol 97, Issue 3.

30. PwC. 2013. *Global Economy Watch,* June (http://www.pwc.co.uk/economic-services/global-economy-watch/summary-june-2013.j html).

31. Data from World Intellectual Property Organisation.

32. Figures from the Centre for Retail Research (http://www.retail research.org/whosegonebust.php).

33. For a more detailed analysis of the challenges facing UK retailers, see A. Sentance, UK retailing: adjusting to the 'New Normal'? (http://

www.sentance.com/the_hawk_talks.htm#Tough times to continue for UK consumers and retailers).

34. *BP Statistical Review of World Energy*, 2013 edn (http://www.bp.com/en/global/corporate/about-bp/statistical-review-of-world-energy-2013.html).

35. The *Oxford English Reference Dictionary* describes dystopia as a 'nightmare vision of society, often as one dominated by a totalitarian or technological state.' Orwell's *1984* and Aldous Huxley's *Brave New World* are cited by the dictionary as examples of dystopian societies.

36. S. D. King. 2013 *When the Money Runs Out: The End of Western Affluence*, p. 7. Yale University Press.

37. The progress of the Japanese automotive industry is well documented in D. T. Jones, D. Roos and J. P. Womack. 1990. *The Machine That Changed the World*. Simon & Schuster.

38. See UK Office for National Statistics, International comparisons of productivity, September 2013.

39. Latest World Bank figures show that female labour force participation for 15+ year olds is 49% in Japan, compared with 58% in US, 56% in the UK and around 60% in Scandinavian economies. Italy is the worst performer in the G7, with just 38% of the 15+ female population active in the workforce.

40. E. Fingleton. 2012. The myth of Japan's failure. *New York Times* Sunday Review, 6 January.

41. Konstantin Chernenko briefly succeeded Andropov in 1984 but led the Soviet Union for only just over a year before Gorbachev took over.

42. *OECD Economic Outlook* No. 93, June 2013.

43. See, for example, PwC *Global Economy Watch* (http://www.pwc.co.uk/economic-services/global-economy-watch/index.jhtml).